ON THE DEEP;

OR,

THE MISSIONARY'S DAUGHTER.

A STORY OF THE PACIFIC OCEAN.

By ROGER STARBUCK,

AUTHOR OF "GOLDEN HARPOON," ETC., ETC.

LONDON:

GEORGE ROUTLEDGE & SONS,

THE BROADWAY, LUDGATE HILL.

ON THE DEEP.

CHAPTER I.

THE FAIR PASSENGER.

THE anchor was atrip; the sails were sheeted and hoisted; the "Stars and Stripes" danced up to the mizzen-gaff; a parting salute was fired, and then, catching the breeze upon her starboard quarter, away she went—the bark Rainbow, of New York—bowling out of the harbour of Maui, Sandwich Islands, homeward bound. Leaning against the weather-rail, stood a young girl of eighteen, Grace Greenville by name, watching the lessening shores with melancholy interest. Her cheek was pale, and tears were in her soft brown eyes; for, fast fading from her gaze, was the little wooden church, behind which lay the recently-buried remains of her father, "the old Missionary." Grace, who had lived with him upon the island ever since her tenth year, was, by his death, left an orphan, her mother having died before he sailed from his native shores. She had taken passage in the Rainbow, in compliance with his last wish that she should sail for New York, and seek her only living relative, her father's sister, who often had written to him that she would be glad of the society of her niece.

But no thought of her aunt, or of her native land, could now find room in the mind of the grief-stricken girl. She was thinking of the little green mound in the churchyard, and of the calm face beneath—the old benevolent face, that so often had smiled upon her in the cottage among the cocoa-nuts. She was leaving them now, never, probably, to see them again. Her tears flowed faster and faster as the familiar shores receded; but the pitiless winds were heedless of her sorrow; they filled the sails, and mockingly whistled among the shrouds. The land grew more and more indistinct; at last it seemed to fade away in a blue mist. Then, stifling a sob, the young girl buried her face in her hands.

Her grief did not escape the attention of the officers. The captain, a plump, weather-beaten old sea-dog, moved toward her, intending to make an effort at consolation; but he was prevented by his first mate, Mr. Block, who confronted him with a solemn shake of the head, and a warning motion of the hand. Never having been married, the skipper had great faith in the knowledge of woman-kind possessed by a man who, like Block, had buried three wives; so, moving on tip-toe to the lee side of the quarter-deck, he beckoned the mate to his side, anxious to learn the cause of his mysterious pantomime, which, he doubted not, was connected with some wonderful secret of the female heart.

It may be as well to state here, that the mate, while exceedingly vain of his knowledge of the gentler sex, prided himself still more upon what he was pleased to term his " 'th'rough' acquaintance with Walker's Dictionary," an old copy of which was always kept upon a shelf near his berth, within easy reach of his hand when he retired. From this volume he was in the habit of committing to memory such lengthy and high-sounding words as, in his opinion, would dignify his conversation, and impress his auditors with the belief that he was a man of profound wisdom and erudition. Unfortunately,

however, he never deemed it necessary to learn the defini
tions of the words selected; and the result of this neglect
was that they were as much out of place in the expressions
he used, as plums would have been in sea-biscuits, or
delicate sauces served up with tough pieces of salt junk.
Their effect was rendered all the more striking by faulty
pronunciation, and by their coming from a mouth twisted
considerably to one side from long and constant use of
the weed. Moreover, the feature was surmounted by a
" club" nose, which divided a pair of hard matter-of-fact
eyes, so accustomed to looking to windward, that every
spark of intellectual fire had been, if I may be allowed
the expression, extinguished by the sea breeze.

Moving his head slowly and mysteriously from side to
side, this worthy now placed one hand upon the captain's
shoulder, and with the other pointed significantly toward
the fair orphan, occasionally opening his mouth as though
about to speak, and then shutting it in an emphatic
manner. Profoundly affected, wrought up to the very
highest pitch of expectation, the skipper at length could
contain himself no longer.

" Out with it," he whispered, eagerly. " Ay, ay,
Block, now is your time—out with it."

" Mark my words, then," responded the mate, " and
mark me well, Captain Capstan. Never, when them
kind is a-worrying, should they be introduced upon. Consequences the most awful might resolve from it. Trying
to smother her affections, she'd sure to break the heart of
her !"

" Why, bless me !—no—you don't say ! God bless the
poor thing !" cried the captain, anxiously. " And Block,"
he added, placing a hand upon the other's wrist, " it's
lucky you're here. I won't give in to any man where

seamanship's consarned, but woman's different—ay, ay, woman's your forty *(forte)* Block !"

The mate bowed with the air of a man to whom compliments of this description were quite familiar. He took the captain's proffered arm, and the two begun to pace the deck, treading very softly, that they might not disturb the young girl.

" I'm struck with the idea," whispered the skipper, " that we ought to contrive in some way—by our dress for a 'sample'—to show our sympathy for this poor orphan. These checked shirts are hardly the thing. What would be the most proper dress, Block ?"

" Something black," responded the mate, emphatically, " we must dress in black—every man of us officers. Black's the badger of mourning—black coats, black vests, black pants, and hats. And we must *wear* our hats, Captain Capstan, so as to have everything in symphony."

" That's all well enough, Block, except about the hats. Blow me if I hardly think—"

" Ay !" interrupted the mate, " that's the most impervious p'int of all. We must wear them hats at the table, Capstan, or all the rest goes for nothing. Your hair is grey, mine is red, and the second mate's is brown, which would be an awful dissembling of gay colours to show to a lass that's just lost her father. Whereas, if they be rendered indivisible by our black hats, we have our badgers of mourning complete. She'll depreciate it all," added Block, with a mysterious gleam in his eyes, " her complex little heart, with all its womanly miseries of affection, is as well known to me as the dictionary."

" You are right—you are right—I do believe !" said Capstan, rubbing his hands. " Your knowledge of the feminine community is wonderful, Block."

"And now," said the latter, "I'll go forward and inform that youngster of our contentions; otherwise he'll be a-rigging himself up, thinking to produce an appreciation upon our orphan."

The youngster spoken of was Guy Loring, the second mate—a hardy, fine looking fellow of twenty-three years, and a native of Nantucket. Though he had spent more than a third of this period at sea, yet he was a very intelligent young man, having devoted every leisure moment to the reading of instructive and entertaining books ; so that he formed an example, by no means uncommon, of an inferior officer better educated than those above him in authority. Men of classical acquirements are often found amongst the foremast hands of war vessels, and sometimes even among the crews of merchantmen. A professor of languages, who, from a love of adventure, had shipped in the Rainbow as a common sailor, had commenced to instruct the second mate in some of the higher branches of knowledge, and, to say the least, there had as yet been no lack either of attention or application on the part of the pupil.

At that moment, however, he could spare no time to think of books. He was superintending the work of lashing the anchor, and stowing the cable—now and then lending a helping hand. Thus engaged, he was not aware of the presence of Block—who had glided forward —until he heard the voice of that worthy behind him.

"You'll wear black at dinner to-day, Mr. Loring, and keep your hair indivisible by means of your beaver, which is not to be taken off at the table."

A marlinespike dropped from Loring's hand to the deck.

He turned and eyed the mate with astonishment.

" Why not, sir ?"

" For symphony," responded Block ; " that poor **girl** needs it, God knows ; being left an orphan, and all alone here among us rough nauticals, not one of which she's ever seen before with the acceptation of Capstan, who was very lightly acquainted with the mushroomery."

" With what, sir ?"

" The missionary," suggested the professor of languages, who just then passed behind the two men, dragging a portion of the cable with his chain-hook.

" Oh ! but why are we to wear our hats, Mr. Block? It seems to me—"

" Because," interrupted the mate, " we must have everything black. It'll have a smoothing influence upon her ; she'll depreciate our delicacy."

So saying he returned to the quarter-deck.

Grace had by this time quitted it, and sought the solitude of her little apartment. She was seated upon a cushioned chair, turning over the leaves of her Bible, and deriving consolation from its pages. Half an hour afterwards she heard a knocking at her door. She opened it to confront the steward, who, in obedience to orders, wore a full suit of black, even to his hat, the crown of which was very high, and shaped something like a pyramid.

" Dinner's ready, Miss," he said, in a mournful voice, " ready and waiting."

She entered the state-room, and took her place at the table. Opposite to her sat the captain and his mate, attired in black broadcloth, with the rims of their beavers pulled down over their eyebrows. The features of both were twisted into an expression of deep solemnity, which seemed wholly out of place on faces so plump and rosy.

The captain did the honours of the table with a gravity in keeping with his melancholy looks; but Grace scarcely tasted of the food put before her. She felt too sad to eat; and yet she could not helping noticing that everybody she saw wore a black suit, and kept his hat on. This surprised her not a little; and she was much perplexed when Block, pulling up the cuffs of his coat, as though about to engage in some pugilistic encounter, addressed her in the following mysterious manner:—

"On the present occasion of consolence, which Capstan and I tender in a way we hope will meet with your fair depreciation, we deign to offer our supreme regrets that Mr. Loring being indisposed to finish a job about the anchor, has not been able to share with us in this convivial symphony, which, it is to be hoped, you'll find delicate."

"You are very kind," said Grace, looking exceedingly puzzled.

"Ay, ay, blow me, Block, but that was a masterly stroke!" cried Capstan, bringing the end of his knife-handle upon the table with great force. "And Miss Greenville," he added, addressing her in a voice of emotion, "we would lay down our lives for you—every man of us! Block, here, whose knowledge of women is wonderful, can divine all your wants, for which we hope to ' previde ' satisfactorily."

"My knowledge of females," said the mate, by way of explanation, "isn't so much the result of insinuation as it is of experiment."

The young girl, after thanking both for their sympathy and good wishes, made her way to the quarter-deck. She looked in the direction of the islands, and saw a mass of dark, sulphurous-looking clouds. She noticed, too, that the wind had nearly died away, and that the sails were flapping heavily against the masts.   Loring, who had come aft to give some order to the man at the wheel, approached her in a deferential manner.

"Miss Greenville," he said, lifting his hat and bowing respectfully, "I hope you will pardon me, a stranger, for speaking to you, but I could never forgive myself were I not to explain the meaning of the singular spectacle you have just witnessed below.   I would not have you think for the world that there is a man in this craft rude enough to wound your feelings intentionally—"

"Oh no, sir," interrupted Grace, with a sweet but melancholy smile, "I know there is not; and I feel very grateful for the kind way in which I have already been treated."

"And yet," said the young man, "you must have been hurt by the seeming want of respect shown by Block and Capstan, in wearing their hats before you at the table."

"Indeed, sir, I was not," she replied. "Though I will not deny that I was surprised. I have no doubt that they had some good reason for keeping their hats on."

Loring then proceeded to explanations, concluding with the earnest assurance that he had tried very hard to persuade the two officers to abandon their ridiculous plan.

Before Grace could reply, a distant noise, like the humming of a swarm of bees, became perceptible.   Turning their eyes toward the mass of clouds to windward, they saw too great columns of hazy vapour rolling round and round, as if upon invisible pivots, and sweeping toward the vessel with great rapidity.   The tops of these gigantic pillars were among the clouds, from which they sloped downward to the sea.   The water beneath and around them was lashed into foam, and the spray could be seen leaping high above the waves, as though it was scooped up by a terrific whirlwind.

The young officer hastily quitted the side of his fair companion.

" Hands by the halliards ! In with royals and to'gallant sails !" he shouted, in a voice that rung through every corner of the bark.

The lighter canvas was clewed in and furled. The fore and mizen topsails were next stowed, after being double-reefed ; and very soon the vessel's canvas was reduced to a close-reefed maintopsail, single-reefed foresail and fore-topmast staysail. By this time every breath of air around the bark seemed to have died away. The atmosphere was almost stifling. There was not a wrinkle in either of the three sails. And yet, not quite a league off the weather-quarter, the approaching tempest raged and howled with terrific fury. The two gigantic pillars had dissolved in the rack and mist of the storm. A far-extending network of driving rain ; torn masses of black vapour, driven hither and thither ; the overhanging clouds, rolling and mingling in dark, sulphurous volumes, and the crests of the waves, whirled into spray by the lashing winds, formed a strange contrast with the clear sky and sunny waters to leeward.

Block and Capstan, who had come on deck while the men were shortening sail, stood near the mizzen-mast, alternately glancing aloft and to windward.

" I don't like the look of that main to'gallant mast and yard," the captain at length said to his mate. " I think you had best send 'em down."

Block gave the required order, and such of the men as were not engaged in lashing the boats, battening down the hatches, &c., &c., darted aloft to obey. Just as the top yard and mast were lowered to the deck, the foremost cloud of the storm passed over the vessel. The rigging hummed like a top; a scarcely perceptible shiver seemed to run through every timber: the three sails filled with a noise like the report of a musket.

"Now, then—steady as you are—there—at—the—wheel!" cried Capstan, in a voice something like the prolonged howl of a wolf.

Whiz-z-z ! — burr-r-r-r !—hoo-oo-oo !—whish-sh-sh !—came the storm, bursting upon the bark with a perfect avalanche of driving rain, and with hurricane gusts that drove Grace into the companion-way, down which she retreated with all possible haste. The stout vessel fell upon her beam ends; her swaying masts creaked complainingly; her timbers groaned as though about to part; torrents of water came pouring over her lee bulwarks; she was hurled, rather than driven, through a vortex of boiling, hissing waves, that threw clouds of spray even to her topsail yards. The maintopsail and the foresail broke loose from their sheets, and after flapping wildly about for a moment were torn to shreds. The foretopmast stays and weather foretopmast shrouds, parting almost simultaneously, the mast went over the side with a loud crash. The maintopmast followed, and immediately afterward down came the mizzen. Men with axes darted forward and aft to clear the wreck, but the bark rolled and plunged so violently, that a long time elapsed before this task was accomplished.

Soon the fury of the tempest begun to abate; the wind, hauling round to the north-east, however still blew a heavy gale, which the captain predicted would last for several days. As he could neither return to the islands nor repair damages during the present state of the weather, he was obliged to set a single-reefed mainsail, and put his vessel before the wind, or on a south-west course. This he pursued for three days, at the end of which time the gale fell away to a light breeze; an occurrence that greatly delighted all hands, who were much exhausted with constant watchfulness and hard work at the pumps.

In the evening, Capstan called his crew aft, and informed them that they should be allowed quarter-watches during the night, as he wanted them to be in good condition at daylight, to begin the work of getting up spare topmasts and yards. The men cheered and went forward, while Loring, who had charge of the first-watch, commenced pacing the quarter-deck. The shadows of night now had settled around the bark; the moon was vailed by leaden-coloured clouds; the gloom was almost impenetrable. The young man, as soon as his brother-officers had gone below, stepped to the binnacle to look at the compass. The vessel still was heading south-west, but not moving faster than at the rate of two or three knots. He walked to the weather-rail, and, leaning carelessly against it, the vision of a sweet young face glided into his mind. It was that of Grace Greenville, which through all the late perils had worn a saint-like expression of resignation and fortitude, varied only by glances of deep sympathy often directed toward the hardy fellows, who, with drenched garments, worked so manfully at the pumps. Fearing, however, that his pleasant reverie might make him forgetful of duty as officer of the watch, the second-mate interrupted it by moving quickly along the lee gangway.

"Tom Green," he shouted to the man on the look-out, "I hope you are wide-awake there?"

No answer was returned, and on gaining the knight-heads Loring discovered that the man was fast asleep—the poor fellow being completely worn out with his late exertions. Under different circumstances, the second mate would have roused the sailor with a rough shake and a sharp reprimand; but he now resolved to allow him to sleep an hour longer before disturbing him. He seated himself upon the spritsail-yard to keep a look-out in his place until the time of grace should have expired. The gloom, as said, was nearly impenetrable; yet, as he glanced off the lee-bow, he thought he could distinguish the outline of some dark object gliding swiftly across the water. It was apparently not far from the vessel, and, to obtain a better view, he sprung to his feet. The object, or rather the outline, now disappeared, and believing either that his imagination had deceived him, or that the vision was nothing more than a large sea-bird, he returned to his seat. At this moment—perhaps influenced by a bad dream—the slumberer on the knight-heads groaned and rolled over upon his back. Loring, who believed that the sailor was suffering from nightmare, roused him at once. The man rose, and, in a confused manner, began an apology for sleeping at his post; but the second mate quietly assured him that he should not punish him on this occasion.

"You will not deprive me of my watch below, nor give me extra work?"

"No."

"Thank you, sir. I will never again close my eyes while on duty, if I die for it."

"That's right, Tom; I know you'll keep your word," answered Guy, as he moved away.

He walked to the binnacle, and a second time looked

at the compass. The vessel was heading steadily upon her course; the trusty helmsman, an old sailor, by the *sobriquet* of Ben Ringbolt, handled the wheel in a manner which gave perfect satisfaction to the officer of the watch. Having exchanged a few remarks with the old man, he stepped to the weather-side of the deck, and seated himself upon the carpenter's chest, facing the forward part of the craft. Not ten minutes had elapsed when he fancied that the vessel's head was falling off. He rose and peered eagerly forward to assure himself that such was the case, being slow to believe that a steersman like Ben would allow the bark to swing even a quarter of a point from her proper course. Very soon, however, his doubts were removed; he turned quickly upon his heel.

"What's the matter there at the wheel? Where are you going to?" he shouted.

There came no response.

The binnacle, which concealed the face of the steersman, was about ten yards from where the second mate stood. He cleared this space with a couple of bounds, and was beginning to address the sailor in an angry manner, when something peculiar in his attitude arrested the words. The old tar stood motionless, with his head bowed upon his breast; with his arms drooping over the wheel. Loring's first thought was that he had been attacked with a fit of apoplexy. He laid him gently upon the deck with one arm, while putting down the wheel with the other; but the next moment a cry of horror escaped him. A handkerchief about the man's neck having become loosened, his throat was revealed covered with blood, and disfigured by an ugly-looking gash near the windpipe!

CHAPTER II.

BLOCK GOES TO RECONSIDER.

THAT the unfortunate man had not inflicted the stab with his own hand, the second mate became convinced, after he had examined the sheath-knife attached to the sailor's belt. This, the only weapon in his possession, showed no trace of blood.

Who, then, was the author of the crime?

Surely no man in the ship, for Ringbolt had been loved and respected by all. There certainly was some strange mystery connected with the deed. It must have been perpetrated in a very stealthy manner, since Loring had known nothing of it until now, though he had been sitting within ten yards of the binnacle. He quitted the spot and summoned the four men of the watch; but they could give him no clue to the fearful secret. They hung over the dead body, lost in speechless astonishment and wonder.

The young man now stationed a sailor at the wheel, and moved toward the companionway, intending to rouse the captain, when he encountered Grace as she came hurriedly from the cabin. She stopped on seeing him, and he placed himself before her, to screen the body of Ringbolt from her view. He noticed that she was pale and agitated, that the hand which she placed upon his arm trembled like a leaf.

"Something has occurred to alarm you," he cried.

"Yes," she replied, with a shudder, "I have seen a face, an evil-looking face, peering at me through the cabin-window."

"How long ago was that?"

"Not more than five minutes. It terrified me so much

that I shrunk back into a corner, where I remained until it had disappeared."

Loring started.

" You are sure that your imagination——"

" Oh ! yes," she interrupted, " I am sure that I was not deceived. I saw the face distinctly by the light of the cabin-lamp. The features, if I mistake not, were those of a Malay."

" Ay, ay, and Ringbolt's murderer," Loring added, mentally ; " this is all strange enough."

He gently drew the young girl within the shadow of the companionway. Still anxious to screen from her gaze the dead body, lying so stark and cold near the binnacle, with the rays of the lamp falling full upon its blood-stained throat. Walking to the rail, he peered into the gloom that covered the sea ; but he saw nothing except the faint outlines of the waves that rippled around the vessel. Had not the darkness partially concealed his face, when he returned to her side, Grace might have seen a troubled, uneasy expression in his eyes.

" Your mysterious visitor will not come again, I trust," he said, with assumed indifference, " as we shall be on the watch for him."

" But why did he come at all ? and can you form any idea from whence he came ?" she inquired.

" To be frank with you," he replied, " I have my suspicions ; it remains to be proved that they are correct."

" And these suspicions ?"

" Miss Greenville," he replied, in a low, earnest voice, " you must pardon me for refusing to express them to you now. Daylight, or perhaps a few hours, will, I think, clear up the mystery."

Though somewhat alarmed, yet she did not pursue her

inquiries. She retired to her apartment, and Loring made his way to the captain's berth.

A sailor is easily waked. Loring's hand had scarcely touched Capstan's shoulder, when he started and opened his eyes. The second mate briefly described what had happened.

"Ben Ringbolt murdered? A face looking in at the cabin-window? Why, bless me lad, here's the dogs to pay!" cried the skipper, springing from his bunk. "You had better wake Block."

The mate was roused, and the three men soon were on deck. After the body of Ringbolt had been wrapped in a blanket and placed on the carpenter's bench in the waist, Capstan moved to the quarter-deck, and motioned his two mates to his side.

"Well, Block, what do you think of this piece of business?"

"It's a mystical proceeding," responded the mate. "In a word, it's a malignant mystery that seems hard to fathom. But it must be invested without delay. You may depend upon it, there's other Malays around besides the one that was seen."

"That's hardly to be disputed," replied Capstan; "and Ringbolt was probably murdered by that villain to prevent his giving the alarm. The rascal must have had a light foot and a quick arm to do this without Loring's seeing or hearing him."

"I have no doubt," said the second mate, "that, if it were not for the darkness, we would see some kind of a vessel—the one to which the murderer belongs—lying not far from our own craft. You doubtless remember that, while we were in the harbour of Maui, the captain of the Spanish brig St. Mary informed us that he had been chased by a suspicious-looking schooner, a few days before his arrival at the island."

"That's logicality!" cried Block, "ay, ay, every word of it. Depend upon it, Loring is right ; and the Malay, I believe, was a sort of scout sent to reconsider us by his cut-throat captain, who saw our light a-shining in the distance, but was, of course, unable to make out our characteristics in the dark."

"In that case, we may expect an attack at any moment," said Capstan, twitching his forelock uneasily. "We must be prepared, Block."

"There's a box of cutlasses in the run," responded the mate ; "besides which we have a few old pikes, two or three muskets, and a couple of revolvers. With them, considerin' that we have twelve good stout fellows in all, we may make some show of persistence."

"That depends upon the number opposed to us," replied the skipper. "We'll fight, however, as hard and as long as we can, for, if our enemies are Malays, we can expect no quarter."

"Not a bit of it," returned Block. "Them fellows have a most superfluous taste for blood. Shall I rouse up the men, sir ? "

"Ay, ay, and get up the arms, and distribute 'em, as soon as possible."

These orders were promptly executed; after which good lookouts were stationed about the ship. Not knowing the exact whereabouts of the suspected craft, Capstan then hauled up his mainsail and lay to. This was scarcely done, when the lookout forward reported a light directly ahead, and apparently about the distance of a league. The skipper looked at it through his night-glass, but the instrument being damaged, afforded him no assistance.

"It's probably the vessel," said Block; "p'r'aps we'd better ware ship and show our heels—that is to say, what little we have left," he added, glancing disconsolately toward the stumps of the three masts.

"No," Capstan answered, decidedly, "we will not wear, for, in my opinion, that light is shown from some boat in order to deceive us. Otherwise, why should it be shown at all ?"

"Light, ho !" cried at this moment one of the lookouts stationed in the after part of the vessel.

"Where away ?" shouted Capstan.

"Off the weather-quarter."

"Another one !" cried Block. "Blow me but there's something incredulously suspicious about that !"

As he spoke, both lights were suddenly extinguished.

"How now, Block? What do you think that means?"

"It's sartainly an anatomical pantomime," responded the mate; "but I think I can resolve it. One of them lights was that of the Malay, adrift in his boat, and the other that of the vessel. They were signalizing to—"

"Light, ho !" shouted another lookout; "right astern, about a league distant."

"A third light !" cried Block and Capstan, in the same breath.

"The rascals are up to some infarnal trick," continued the skipper, "and I'd give considerable to know what it is."

He gazed steadily toward the light, until it was suddenly extinguished.

"A boat should be sent to reconsider," said the mate. "They may be a-preparing some kind of a trap for us. If you say the word, I'll take the cutter and go."

"Ay, ay, that's a good idea. But be careful, Block,

be careful. We haven't any men to lose. They must put their arms in the boat, and must muffle their oars."

These orders were obeyed, after which the little craft was cautiously lowered. Four men, who had been selected for the crew, then took their places, and, carefully plying their oars, the boat glided off into the darkness.

Block steered toward that quarter in which the last light—the one astern—had been seen. Owing to the precautions taken, the boat made but little noise : the mate issued his orders in whispers ; there was no conversation among the men. They had proceeded in this manner for about a quarter of an hour, when Block suddenly leaned forward and peered eagerly ahead. He fancied he could distinguish the outline of some object at no great distance. He was soon enabled to make out the form of a man seated in a canoe, and he doubted not that this was Ringbolt's murderer—the Malay. He ordered his men to pull more softly, and turning his head at the same instant, the occupant of the canoe saw the approaching boat. He seized his paddles and urged his light craft through the water with extraordinary swiftness.

"Ay, ay, there he goes !" cried Block, "a-running away from us. A 'guilty conscience makes cowards of all.' Pull ahead, lads, long, strong, and steady ; we'll soon have him under our jurisprudence."

The men laid back to their oars with a will, and the boat flew swiftly on in the wake of the fugitive.

Having had the start of his pursuers, however, and his vessel being much lighter than theirs, it was some time before the distance between them began to diminish. The course pursued by the mate soon brought the bark's lantern some distance off his starboard quarter—that is to say, nearly opposite to the right side of his boat. It struck him that the Malay did not now put forth so much exertion as he had previously done, and believing that exhaustion was the cause, he encouraged his men with hopes of a speedy termination of the chase.

"Pull ahead, lads—pull ahead! A few more strokes, and the criminality will be in our possession."

The men strained every muscle—the boat flew onward with arrowy speed; it was soon within a few feet of the canoe.

The mate now ordered his men to jump up and stand by, to seize the Malay. Placing their oars apeak, they sprang from their thwarts to obey, but before they could turn, the fugitive, uttering a peculiar cry, directed his canoe to one side, and the boat shot past it.

Directly ahead of him, Block then heard the heavy splashing of oars, and made out the scarcely perceptible outlines of human figures.

A clear, musical voice greeted his ears the next moment.

"Boat, ahoy! if you try to escape us it will be the worse for you!"

He remained for a few seconds speechless with astonishment: the men stood motionless, waiting for orders.

"Ay, ay," cried the mate at last, as he caught sight of nearly twenty forms seated in a longboat, "bless me, if this ain't a wonderful dispensary of Providence, the meeting with them villains in this unexpected manner. Down men!—down to your oars, and pull like thunderbolts!"

The crew needed no second bidding. They seized their

oars—the mate whirled the boat's head toward the bark—and away they went. Turning his head, Block saw the canoe moving toward the other boat. A moment later, the crashing of small arms was heard, and a shower of leaden missiles flew about the heads of himself and his crew.

"Stretch to your oars, men! Stretch for your lives! Another volley, and some of you may be sent to the everlasting 'bosom of destruction!' Spring my blades! spring with a will!"

A few minutes afterward, he looked behind him again, when, to his surprise, he could see nothing of his pursuers, though the dip of their oars was audible off his quarter. Believing that they had given up the chase, he ordered his men to "slacken" their exertions, and pull a long easy stroke.

"I must presarve your muscle, my lads," said he, "as much as I can, for I think you'll need it, eloquently, in a few hours."

"Beg pardon, sir," said old Tom Rocket, the bow oarsman, "but it seems to me that them rascals are a-trying to head us off—to get between us and the bark. The sound of their oars was off our quarter a minute ago—it's now off our bow."

Block inclined his head to one side, and listening attentively soon concluded that the man was right; so he again ordered the crew to put forth all their strength at the oars. They had not proceeded far, however, when the shadowy outlines of the longboat and its occupants were seen directly ahead, and approaching rapidly.

"Ay, ay, we're cut off from our craft now, sure enough," growled the mate, as he whirled the boat round, "but we'll make them cut-throats respire a little before they come up with us. So spring ahead, men—spring ahead !"

The course now pursued by the two boats, carried them toward the quarter where the first light had been seen. The mate's crew strained every muscle, but it soon became evident that their pursuers were fast gaining on them. In the course of half an hour, the two boats were not more than nine or ten yards apart, and Block was preparing a whole "volley" of learned words to discharge at the Malays, when, not far ahead, looming up through the gloom, he saw the outlines of masts and yards.

"Luff up there aboard the schooner, and lie to?" was shouted from the pursuing boat, in the same musical voice that previously had startled Block and his men, " I'll put some prisoners aboard, directly, to be strung up at the yard-arm !"

Some moments elapsed before the order was obeyed, by which time the schooner had forged so far ahead, that in luffing up, she came between the two vessels, bringing her own boat abreast the starboard main rigging, and the other directly beneath her fore-chains, on the larboard, or opposite side. The mate was not slow to take advantage of this manœuvre. Hearing the sound of the oars of his pursuers, as they pulled round the schooner's stern to seek him, he directed the cutter toward her bows, and crossed them, thus getting far ahead of the longboat, on a course that led him toward the Rainbow.

" Ay, ay, we've just sarved 'em an indigenous trick," cried Block, as the shouts and yells of rage from his foes were borne to his ears. There's nothing like intrigue, my lads. If they catch us now, I'm willing to swing for it !"

For some reason or other the schooner did not join in the pursuit, and the crew of the longboat gave up the chase when the fugitives were within half a mile of the bark.

CHAPTER III.

A FIGHT IN THE DARK.

"WE are sartainly in a bad fix!" said Capstan, after his mate had described to him the result of his expedition. "How many men do you think that schooner can muster for an attack?"

"About thirty; and when we're 'attackled,' it will probably be by two boats' crews, to say nothing of the peppering we'll get from the guns of the vessel, for, in my opinion, she has a few guns aboard."

"And we have nothing of that sort except an old eight-pounder," growled Capstan. "That gale was a bad thing for us, Block, as it's crippled us so we can't escape. I haven't any doubts that we'll have to fight before morning."

"Ay, ay, sir, and its pretty easy to interrogate the result. Them dusky rascals will show us no quarter. They have a most intrinsic taste for blood. - They'd cut a dozen throats for the sake of an old piece of copper, or a few nails."

"We must try to avoid an attack as long as we can," said the skipper, "and something may turn up in our favour; another craft, perhaps, which may consent to assist us, and—"

"But how can this be done?" queried the mate.

"By getting up jury masts at once. We have plenty of spare spars and canvas. We may contrive, in this way, to edge off some considerable distance from the schooner in the dark."

" A good plan, 'previding' we can do this without being discovered," returned Block, "but that canoe humbug is, I dare say, even now somewhere on the lookout."

" We will try at any rate, and see what we can do !"

Accordingly, all hands, with the exception of the lookouts, were set to work. The ship's lanterns afforded such poor light, however, that it was a long time before the first spar was hoisted to the stump of the mainmast. Just as the men were preparing to secure it, a bright flash was seen off the lee bow ; a loud report followed, and the next moment a ten-pound shot went howling over the heads of the sailors.

" Confound the rascals," growled Block, between his set teeth, " I thought things would turn out in this way. There's an end to our getting up jury-masts, Captain Capstan. They've been reconsidering us again, and know what we're about."

" Ay, ay," roared Capstan, savagely; " and they're a sneaking pack of thieves. If I had a few more men, I'd venture to board and carry the schooner !"

" Good !" exclaimed the professor of languages, who had been stationed near the tackle to help hoist the spar, " very good !"

As he spoke, he wound an old red comforter tightly about his wasp-like waist, and emphatically tapped the handle of his cutlass.

In addition to the comforter, he wore patched duck trowsers, a red shirt, and an old smoking-cap, which articles he thought gave him something of the air of a piratical desperado. His shipmates might have thought so too, had not his figure borne some resemblance to a pair of tongs. His nose was not very warlike, either, being curved like a trumpet, and bridged by a pair of green spectacles.

Capstan looked at him with a grim smile.

"I tell you what it is, my man," he said, in a gruff voice, "don't let me catch you shirking when we come to close quarters with them cut-throats; I rather think you've got too much l'arning to be very spunky?"

"*Nous verrons!*" cried the professor, gnashing his teeth ferociously; "yes, sir, only give me a chance, and we shall see!"

"Ay, ay, Capstan, 'new-for-wrong' is the word!" exclaimed Block, in a mournful voice. "I wouldn't have thought that you'd have made sich an insinuation upon us that happen to have a little extra l'arning, and I repeat that it's a decisive 'new-for-wrong!'"

Before the skipper could frame a reply, there followed another flash, another report, and a second shot was heard as it struck the bark alongside of her cutwater, just as her bows were lifted by a swell. The ball went crashing through her timbers, and with a roaring noise the water poured through the opening thus made.

"She's a gone case, now!" cried Capstan—"the poor little Rainbow! She'll soon go down, and the only consolation is that them fellows have bit off their own noses! Get all the provision, and as many other useful articles into the boats as you can, Block."

He spoke calmly, but the moisture gathered in his eyes as he looked round the decks of a craft in which he had performed many a good voyage. The boats, two in number, consisting of the launch and the cutter, were ready for lowering by the time Grace Greenville, who had been informed by Loring of what had happened, came up from the cabin. The young man took his place by her side, and cheered her with hopeful words, for he knew that she felt more alarm than she expressed.

The ship was settling fast; her bulwarks forward were already partially submerged. Capstan gave the order to lower away. The boats struck the water simultaneously; after Grace had been helped to a comfortable seat which the second mate had prepared for her in the cutter, they were manned.

"Pull ahead!" was next ordered, and the two vessels were pushed from the side of the sinking bark.

"Quite an adventure, this," remarked the professor of languages, "it will make an interesting item for my journal."

"The less said about that, Green Specs, the better," growled an old sea-dog, who pulled the cutter's midship oar. "I've seen you take that log-book from your shirt-bosom more than once to-night; but you may have some 'hightems' pretty soon, mate, of a sort that you'll never have a chance to put down!"

"I doubt it," returned the professor, "I prophesy that I shall live to have my journal published."

"Never mind about your jarnal, Quill," cried Capstan, "but just mind your stroke!"

"Ay, ay, sir," replied Quill; but even as he spoke, his oar, slipping from his grasp, threw him backward from his thwart.

Before the skipper could give way to the anger excited by this "lubberly" accident, a succession of fierce yells and imprecations from the bark caused him to turn his head. The outlines of the vessel were still faintly visible, and a number of lanterns, moving to and fro about her decks, proclaimed that she was already boarded by the sea-robbers.

"Howl on, you infarnal villains!" roared Capstan. "Them shrieks of yours are as music to my ears, for they show that you are baffled. You'll get no plunder out of the poor little Rainbow!"

He had scarcely concluded when the Malays were heard dropping into their boats. These, two in number, were distinguished a moment later darting in the wake of the bark's crew. Grace shuddered with terror; the boat-lanterns revealed the ashy paleness of her features. Involuntarily she drew closer to Loring's side.

"Have no fear," said he, "we might give 'em a lengthy chase, but they'll not pursue us very long. They will soon return to the schooner."

"And then the schooner will chase us, will it not?"

"Doubtless; but I dare say we will contrive to elude her in the dark."

"God help us all!" murmured the young girl. "It is dreadful, Mr. Loring, for your men to have to work so hard after the fatigues they have already undergone."

"Men under circumstances like the present, Miss Greenville, do not feel the effects of the very hardest kind of work until it is over, and—"

A crash was heard; a flash lighted for an instant the dark faces of the Malays in the foremost of the pursuing boats; a volley of bullets whizzed about the heads of the cutter's crew. One of the missiles severed a lock of the young girl's hair and grazed her temple.

Loring sprung from his thwart, and stood behind her to shield her person with his own form.

"No, no, I will not permit that!" she cried, anxiously, "sit down again, I implore you, or you will certainly get shot!"

The second mate smiled.

"I beg your pardon," said he; "but I shall disobey you this time. I don't think you need be alarmed, however, those fellows are miserable marksmen; besides which, the darkness is in our favour. I hardly think they will fire again. Ah!" he added, as a roaring, gurgling noise was heard astern, and the bark's lantern suddenly seemed to dive out of sight in the water. "There she goes, the noble Rainbow—she has made her last plunge!"

Capstan sighed heavily, and clenched his fists.

"Ah! but I'd like to have it in my power to sarve the schooner the same trick!" he cried, in a deep, but passionate voice.

"Good!" cried Professor Quill, "remarkably good!"

"How many men," continued Capstan, addressing his mate, "should you say are in that foremost boat?"

Block, who was seated in the stern-sheets of the launch which was now dashing along within a few yards of the boat, replied, without hesitation:—

"Ten; not a soul more. I contracted 'em by the flash of their arms when they fired!"

"Your men in the launch have their cutlasses with 'em, have they not?"

"Ay, ay, sir!"

The professor, as though struck with a suspicion of what was passing through the captain's mind, eagerly turned round, his green spectacles flashing in the light of the boat-lantern. Some minutes elapsed before the skipper again spoke. He then ordered the launch alongside of the cutter. Block obeyed; and, motioning to Loring to follow him, the captain leaped into the boat. The second mate was soon by his side. The captain then informed Block that he intended to make a dash at the pirates' foremost boat.

"I'm of opinion that it'll be a useless ambassadorship," returned the first officer. "Two boats ag'in one—"

"No," interrupted Capstan, "the boat is so far ahead of the one astern that it won't get any assistance from its companion during the fight. I think I can wind up the combat before the rear boat comes up. Jump in here—four more men from the cutter!" he added, turning toward the crew of that vessel.

Up sprung the professor of languages, but before he could advance a step, four of his shipmates had leaped into the launch.

"Oh, my!" exclaimed Quill, much disappointed, "this is really too bad! Don't you want another man, captain? You'll find me quite serviceable—you will, really."

"Them spectacles of your'n are too 'valleble' to get smashed," returned Capstan, "so you'd better stay where you are."

"I am to go with you, of course," said Block, as the skipper, motioned him toward the cutter. "Surely you don't intend to leave me behind?"

"Ay, ay, you must take charge of the other boat."

"I'd rather make one of your party," answered Block. "Why not let Loring stay with the cutter. It strikes me that this is another 'new-for-wrong!'"

"I can't take you," returned the captain, decidedly. "Your knowledge of womankind makes it necessary, of a sartinty, that you, of all others, shouldn't get hurt. Miss Greenville needs somebody that 'surmises' her, and you're the man, Block—ay, ay, you're the man."

"My knowledge of woman isn't to be imputed," said Block, bowing low to Grace; "and, of course, much as I'd like to commingle in the fray, I'm bound to be observant to the wishes of them that requires me."

C

So saying, he stepped into the cutter, and, whirling the head of the launch around, Capstan ordered his men to pull. Away went the boat with arrowy speed, and, in a few minutes, it was within a fathom of the one occupied by the astonished Malays.

"Now, then, lads!" gritted the skipper, through his teeth, "now, then, stand up!"

The stout fellows put their oars apeak, and drawing their cutlasses, obeyed.

A volley was fired from the small-arms of the pirates, and with inexpressible anguish, Capstan saw two of his men fall dead.

The next moment, the bows of the launch dashed full against the side of the other boat, and being lashed to it, a desperate fight ensued. Having sprung into the vessel occupied by their foes, the men of the Rainbow gave them no time to reload, but dealt their blows rapidly and with deadly effect.

Loring had cut down one of the dusky villains, and crossed swords with another, when a gigantic fellow, who wore a red skull-cap and was stripped to the waist, seized him by the nape of the neck, and raised his long knife to inflict a deadly stab. Capstan, however, saw the movement in time to run his cutlass through the giant's body before he could execute his purpose. The man tumbled into the water with a groan, which was echoed by his shipmates. He was evidently an officer, and his fall discouraged them. They retreated over the stern of their craft into the water, leaving the white men masters of their boat, though they (the pirates) still clung to the gunwales. At the same moment Capstan caught sight of the Malays' other vessel speeding rapidly toward him. He sprung into the cutter with the remnant of his crew, now amounting to but six men—the rest having been slain; and, cutting the lashings, ordered the men to pull ahead. They did so; and as they receded from the boat in which they had fought, they saw only four of the villains crawl into it."

"Ay, ay," said old Tom Rocket, "we have l'arned them fellows a lesson that they won't easily forget. There's nothing like makin' strong impressions on them that you meet."

"You are right enough there, Tom," said Capstan; "we've given 'em a blow which will prevent 'em from chasing us much longer in boats."

Peering through the gloom, as he spoke, he was just able to distinguish the dark outlines of the pursuing craft and its occupants.

"They stick to us yet," cried Tom Rocket, "but it ain't because they are anxious-like as to the state of our 'healths.' Nothin' would please 'em better than to run us up to the yard-arm, in which, hows'ever they'll be mighty disapp'inted."

"Ay, that they will," cried the skipper. "But pull ahead, lads, pull ahead. We haven't any time to lose!"

The brave fellows, assisted by the second mate, who worked the after oar, obeyed with such hearty good will, that they were soon alongside of the cutter. The captain, in a few brief words, gave his mate an account of the combat, after which the crews of both boats were equalized. Then Block took his proper place in the launch, while Loring and the skipper entered the cutter.

"Pull ahead," was the next order, and the two vessels flew through the waves.

"Cheer up, Miss Greenville!" exclaimed Loring, as he looked astern; "our pursuers have vanished. They have given up the chase and have returned to the schooner."

"I am glad of that," said she; "but it is dreadful to think that the lives of some of your men have been sacrificed. I would that we had escaped without—"

"That's always the way with the women, I believe,' interrupted Capstan, smiling; "they are always for having everything settled without bloodshed—bless their pugnacious eyes!"

"You are corrective enough there, Captain Capstan," cried Block, from the launch, "and them women that's otherwise is an indigenous species of monster that isn't to be moderated. The three Mrs. Blocks was as gentle as lambkins."

"Ay, ay, beggin' your pardon," cried Tom Rocket, "and sich frisky little creaturs as some of 'em are; some of the lasses I mean, that's to be seen ashore! Why, bless my old eyes, it's the wonderfulest thing in the world that I never got spliced!"

"You may feel congratulative that you never did," exclaimed Block, "for the partner of your woes might have been torn from your depreciative bosom, and extinguished as mine have been, leaving me to mourn for 'em, like the raven, as I've heard of, which always was a-saying 'Nevermore!'"

"Why, now—me! but that's too bad!" cried Capstan, considerably touched—"that's a melancholy 'doxology,' Block, and I feel for you!"

"Ay, ay, but we must try not to mourn for them that's gone," returned the mate. "We must try, instead, to consolidate them that's living. And so," he added, turning toward the young girl, "you will admit me to say, by way of smoothing your sorrows of them that's been slain, that if the attackle hadn't been consummated, we'd have all been captured and deteriorated into mince-meat!"

"My only regret," exclaimed the professor of languages, "is, that it was not in my power to make one of the fighting party. You missed me, I dare say, Captain Capstan?"

"Perhaps we'd have missed you all the same had you been there?" answered the skipper. "So it can make no great difference."

"Why, why, sir. Really now, you don't mean to cast an imputation upon my courage?"

"As you like," answered Capstan bluntly; "perhaps I do!"

"Oh, dear me!" cried the professor, "this is too bad! I am not very pugnacious I know, but to be called a coward before a young lady—"

"I don't think the captain meant that, professor!" good-naturedly interrupted Loring; "he probably meant to imply that you'd be the first man killed; therefore, the first one missed."

"And he'd have been killed," the skipper gruffly added, "because his l'arning wouldn't have left him any spunk—any backbone to help himself."

"Another 'new-for-wrong'" cried Block. "Ay, ay, there you go again, Captain Capstan. I hope you don't think that my l'arning has detrementalized from my persistent qualities."

From some cause or other the professor's spectacles now begun to rattle, while Capstan replied:—

"You've had your trial more than once, Block, so that there's no doubts about you; besides which, your l'arning is of that kind which relates to feminines."

"And the dictionary, Capstan—the dictionary, which

I've perambulated through and through, so that I'm parfectly acquainted with them words which are most voluble
and insinuating."

Another rattle from the green spectacles.

Capstan remained silent.

CHAPTER IV.

THE CHASE NOT YET GIVEN UP.

Soon afterwards, Grace, who had scarcely closed her
eyes for two nights, dropped into a deep slumber, much to
the satisfaction of Loring, who had prepared for her a
snug resting-place near the stern-sheets. Seated upon a
couple of chair-cushions in the bottom of the boat, with
her head reposing on soft pillows spread over a thwart,
she slept as soundly and as peacefully as a child in its
cradle. The light of the boat's lantern, which was now
placed in a position that would prevent the crew of the
schooner from seeing it, fell upon her innocent face, as
though it loved to repose there. It shed a golden tint
upon the threads of her rich brown hair; softly defined
the marble whiteness of her forehead, and the feathery
shadows of her long, drooping eyelashes.

"Gently, lads, gently, with them oars," whispered
Capstan to his crew. "Be careful of your strokes now;
our little girl sleeps."

An order hardly necessary, for these rough men, at the
moment the young girl closed her eyes, had stopped conversing, and had placed bits of cloth in their rowlocks, so
as not to disturb her slumber. Owing to these precautions she did not wake until the shadows were beginning to fade from sea and sky. By this time the breeze
had freshened, and the crew of each boat having rigged a

sail, were, with the exception of the officers, stretched across their thwarts, enjoying a brief season of repose. The sails being expansive, sent the boats gliding through the water at the rate of five or six knots. Both were steering upon a south-west course, which, at their present rate of sailing, would carry them—according to the skipper's calculations—within sight of land before noon that day.

"I hope you slept well, Miss Greenville," said the second mate, "though it must be owned that the accommodation was none of the best."

"I don't think I should have slept better," she answered, smiling, "in the best of beds. Do you think we will see a sail, before long?"

"We may possibly fall in with some whale-ship, as we are not far from one of the cruising grounds. But, at any rate, we shall see land before many hours."

"Oh! I am glad of that!"

An exclamation from Capstan, who stood with his glass pointed astern, drew towards him the earnest eyes of the young girl.

"Ay, ay," he continued, "there she is, the schooner, not much more than a league distant."

He passed the glass to Loring.

"It's a schooner, certainly," said the young man, after a moment's survey; "and there can be no doubt that it is the pirate. But to make sure, we might question Block."

The mate's boat was a few fathoms astern. Capstan hailed it; then slackened his sheet until it had come alongside.

Block took the proffered glass and levelled it towards the vessel.

"That's her!" he cried, the next moment, "that's the rascal in chase of us!"

Grace turned pale and trembled.

The slumberers in both boats were roused, and ordered to take to their oars; and though their arms ached with their previous exertions, yet they obeyed without a murmur. The sight of the lovely, uncomplaining girl, who had shown so much sympathy for them, and who depended upon them for protection, added to their strength.

Very soon, the morning light dissipated every shadow; the schooner could now be seen with the naked eye. Capstan swept the horizon in every direction, with his glass, in the hope of "sighting" some vessel which might be signalled and brought to his assistance, but in vain.

Meanwhile, the pursuing vessel, which had crowded canvas in the chase, gained upon the fugitives every moment; it was soon less than a league astern.

"Loring," whispered Capstan, "this is a bad business. It makes my heart bleed to think of that poor girl's falling into the hands of them bloodthirsty dogs. I see no hope of our escaping 'em!"

"Ay, ay," the second mate sadly replied, "our prospects look dark enough. Though we will all fight for Miss Greenville while we have power to wield a cutlass, yet we must be overpowered at last."

"That's so, lad; and it's awful to think of what will be her fate when she's captured. It's a hard, hard thought to bear, especially as I saw her father a few days before he died; and when he asked me if it would be safe for his daughter to sail in my craft, I told him for a sartainty that it would—that nothing would happen to her! It wasn't right of me to feel so sartain—no, no, it wasn't."

"Matters may not turn out so bad as we think they

will," said Loring, as he directed a steady glance to windward. "There is still room for hope."

Grace heard the concluding words, and her face brightened.

"Thank God ! You really think there is hope for us ?"

"I do."

"What is it, lad ? What do you see ?" inquired the captain, noticing the steadiness of his gaze.

"A fog-bank," answered Loring, "and if this breeze holds long enough, the fog may spread around us in time to enable us to elude the schooner."

Capstan rubbed his hands.

"You are right, my lad," said he, "there is some chance of that. Unless I'm much mistaken, that fog will be upon us in the course of half an hour. If we can contrive to keep a reasonable distance from the craft during that time, I trust we shall be able to lead her on a wrong scent."

He turned briskly toward the mate and ordered him to rig out some more spare pieces of canvas, plenty of which was in both vessels.

"No matter how it's done, Block," he added, "so long as you catch the wind,"

The mate promptly obeyed, and the two boats were soon gliding along under clouds of additional canvas that certainly gave them an odd appearance.

"This is highly 'picturesque,'" remarked the professor, as he turned up his green spectacles to survey the sails. "Highly 'picturesque !' We look like miniature vessels of war. I must make a note of this in my journal !"

"Ay, ay !" cried Block, "it's quite a 'metamoramasis.' We wouldn't hardly know each other at a disrespectful distance."

" There's nothing warlike about it, hows'ever, as the professor seems to think," remarked Tom Rocket, " seeing as we hain't got any ' teeth' to show."

" My dear young lady !" exclaimed Block, looking sternly with one eye at the old seaman, and trying to smile with the other at Grace, " don't let that remark of Tom's incommodate you. By teeth, he means guns, which bears no sort of resemblance to them little ingenious ivories of your'n."

Just then a puff of smoke issued from the schooner's bow; a dull report followed, and a ten-pound shot, plunging into the water within a fathom of the cutter's stern, sent the spray flying over Loring's head.

" Hip ! hip ! hip ! hooray ! hooray !—this is really exciting !" exclaimed the professor of languages, springing to his feet, and waving his smoking-cap about his head.

" Down ! down to your oar !" thundered Capstan; " what kind of boy's play is that ?"

" Beg pardon," cried Quill, " but I couldn't help it; really—I—"

" We'll see how you'll act when it comes to the p'int !" interrupted the skipper sternly ; " none of your boy's play then, or I'll run you through with my own hand."

" You may do so if I don't do my duty," answered Quill. " Oh ! dear me !—yes, indeed !"

Another puff of smoke from the schooner; another shot. It passed through the head of one of the men in the launch. He fell from his thwart with a short, sharp cry.

Grace shuddered, and pressed her hands upon her eyes.

" Poor fellow !" cried the professor, with real feeling. " He died at the post of duty, and shall be praised, as he deserves to be, in my journal !"

"Overboard with him, men," said Block, "we have no time now for a funeral requiem."

Accordingly, the dead body was gently dropped into the sea.

"There goes one of our best men," said Loring, in a mournful voice. "He had a mother and sisters at home, too."

"Ah! it is dreadful!" faltered Grace, with tears in her eyes; "his poor mother! his poor mother!"

"Be consolidated, I beg of you," said Block. "The sufferings of the mother won't endure for a long time. She's old, and will soon join her son in the fields of martyrdom."

"Where we must all go to, sooner or later," put in Tom Rocket. "So dry your eyes, my dear lass, and keep that consolin' thought in your mind."

"Ay, ay; but blow me if I think it's a very consoling one, either, to a young lady in her teens," cried Capstan, "though it may do on a pinch."

"If I've said anything wrong," said Rocket, with an expression of deep concern upon his broad, honest face, "I beg the lady's pardon. I was a-thinking of the blessin's of Christianity when I spoke."

"This isn't a fit time for a moralizing biography," exclaimed Block, "with that schooner a-comin' up hand over fist. She isn't two-thirds of a league from us now."

"God help the girl if she falls into the hands of those demons!" muttered Capstan, with a shudder.

"Yonder comes the fog!" cried Loring, hopefully "The wind is freshening every moment. We'll soon be hidden by the mist."

"I don't know, lad, I don't know!" responded Capstan,

shaking his head. "I'm sartin it'll come just a minute too late."

Block, overhearing this speech, carefully scrutinized the fog-bank, the outer edge of which was now about a mile astern of the schooner, and he mentally acknowledged that the skipper was right. On reflecting a moment, a sudden idea occurred to him which he lost no time in expressing to his commander.

The reader will please bear in mind that the two boats and the schooner were heading directly before the wind. In order, therefore, to prevent the capture of both boats, the mate proposed that the cutter should be kept off on the starboard tack, and the launch on the opposite or larboard. The sails could be easily trimmed to enable the crews to accomplish this manœuvre, which Block had no doubt would result in the escape of the boat containing Grace Greenville. The schooner's foreyards being braced a little to larboard, he had good reason to believe that her captain would keep off for the launch, instead of taking the trouble to brace on the other tack for the sake of capturing the cutter. Before the launch could be taken, the skipper's boat would have been left far astern of the pirates' vessel, and have become shrouded in the fog.

"Ay, ay," replied Capstan, when Block had concluded, "it's the only alternative left us—the only one. As we can't save both boats, it's proper that we should sacrifice the launch to save the cutter, which has in it this precious freight of womankind that you, Block, understand so well. I'll consent to it on the condition that you take my place, while I take yours. Them as old as I am don't mind being cut out of the last few years of their lives; but you, Block—you are still young enough to splice with a fourth wife, and blow me if I desart you! Besides," he added, mournfully, " My old heart is with the Rainbow, which I've sailed for so many years, and which has gone to the bottom of the sea, never more to return. So, come on, Block—come on, old chum, and take my place."

" If I do, may I be dissolved ! " cried the mate. " No —no—I can never consent to your deposition. I've braved death many a time, Capstan, and I ain't afraid of him now, let him exterminate me in whatever capacious manner he chooses ! "

The two boats were now so close that the starboard gunwale of the one, and the larboard of the other, almost touched. Capstan had placed his foot upon that of the cutter, intending to jump into the launch and push the mate into the stern sheets of the other boat, when Loring, with a sudden but gentle motion of his powerful arm, pushed the skipper aside. Then he sprang into the launch, and seizing the tiller with one hand dexterously pushed Block into the cutter. Before either the astonished mate or his superior could utter a word, the receding boat was full five fathoms distant, running along on the larboard tack, her crew having already set and trimmed her sails.

" Good-bye, Capstan ! Good-bye, Block ! Good-bye, Miss Greenville ! " shouted the young officer, smiling and waving his disengaged hand.

" Avast there, Loring ! " roared the mate, jumping up and down in a excited manner. " Come back here, come back at once, I command you, sir ! "

But the second mate, who was now almost beyond hearing distance, only shook his head.

" Ay, ay, Block," said Capstan, " you see it's no use. He always was a sort of headstrong youngster. But, he's lost now—we'll have to let him go. He's acted against

orders—he has, decidedly, though it was done from good
motives. Well, well, there's no help for it."

"I don't see as there is," answered Block, mournfully,
"but I never knew before that it would be so hard to
give up commingling with them that's gone to their
diurnal rest! I had made up my mind to it, d'ye see,
Capstan, and was ready and willing for death."

"And beggin' your pardon," cried Tom Rocket, "you
may not be disapp'inted after all. There's no knowing
what may come to pass."

With wild eyes and pale cheeks, Grace Greenville rose
to her feet, and laid a trembling hand upon the captain's
arm.

"You are not going to desert him !" she faltered.

"There is no other alternative," replied Capstan. "We
must save you, my dear girl, at all hazards."

"No, no!" she cried, firmly. "I am not afraid to die.
For God's sake don't let my presence interfere with any
plan you might wish to adopt. Let no lives be sacrificed
on my account. You must not desert your second mate !
No—no—you must not desert him."

But Capstan shook his head; the sails were trimmed,
and the boat glided off upon the starboard tack, rapidly
increasing the distance between it and the launch.

"I must disobey you, my child," said the old skipper,
sadly. "You can form no idea of what would be your
fate should those barbarians get you in their clutches. If
you were not with us, there would be more lives sacrificed
than there will be now, for then we should all—all of us
rough fellows—stick together, and fight it out until every
one of us was cut to pieces."

"Ah ! my God ! and he—Mr. Loring, together with the
three men with him, must then be killed and slaughtered

without mercy! Tell me—oh, tell me, that there is some hope of their escape!"

"Leave her to me," whispered Block, just as Capstan was about framing a reply, "leave her to me, old chum. You are not the man for them kind. That cutting to pieces of yourn was an invincible blunder, and should never be used in the ears of females, as it has to them a most distressing intimation."

So saying, the mate turned to Grace with a low bow.

"Miss Greenville," said he, hoping to win her confidence and respect by a single skilful stroke, "I have buried three wives!"

She looked up at him with no little astonishment.

"Ay, ay, Miss, and," he added, glancing triumphantly toward the captain, "one of them wives was the very inflection of your fair self, by which you can understand that my apprehension of your nature is complete. Sich being the statement of affairs, I consider it my duty to console you as speedily as possible, which may be done by the informal notice to you that your presence here, instead of causing an excessive diffusion of blood, ameliorates from the same in a manner at once merciful and angelic."

Grace looked puzzled; Capstan nodded admiringly; the green spectacles of Professor Quill rattled violently.

"It's done," whispered Block, in Capstan's ear; "it's done; just look at her!"

She was sitting with clasped hands, pale cheeks, and tear-dimmed eyes, gazing after the receding boat.

The skipper grasped the mate's hand.

"You are a treasure, Block!"

"Not a sob, not a word of grief from her, you perceive."

"Ay, ay, Block, it was a masterly stroke, and God will bless you for it !"

Bang ! from the schooner, and the spiteful whiz of another shot was heard as it passed over the cutter.

"Hooray ! hooray ! hooray !" screamed the professor of languages, "this is exciting !"

"Silence !" roared Capstan. "Don't let me hear you again !"

"Oh, dear me, certainly not !"

"There she goes in chase of the launch !" cried Block. "God help our brave lads !"

The cutter was soon more than a league distant off the schooner's quarter, and only one of the topsails of the launch was now visible to the naked eye, apparently about a mile ahead of the pursuing vessel. Suddenly, the report of a gun was again heard, and the little speck of canvas immediately disappeared. The captain looked through his glass, but he saw no vestige of the boat. An expression of pain passed over his face ; he whispered to his mate, and the latter breathed a heavy sigh. The schooner continued running along on the same course for ten minutes longer, when she braced her yards to starboard, and came round in chase of the cutter. By this time, however, the boat was partially shrouded by the fog ; a few moments later, this became so dense that Capstan felt satisfied that he was screened from the view of his pursuers. He trimmed his sails anew ; then veering, came up to the wind on the starboard tack, and stood away, with the water breaking over both gunwales. He continued upon this course until a sufficient time had elapsed for the schooner to pass to leeward of him, when he again put the cutter before the wind.

"I think we are in a fair way to give that rascal the

slip now," said he; "I should feel cheerful, almost happy, Block, if it were not for the sad fate of Loring and his crew. I am pretty sartin that the boat was stove by that last shot."

"Ay, ay, and we may feel sartin that the schooner didn't pick up our poor fellows that were left struggling in the water. There was only two of 'em that could swim, Loring and Tom Pool, the bow oarsman."

Grace started and sprung to her feet.

"Who knows?" she exclaimed, eagerly. "Perhaps these two men are even now clinging to oars, or to a piece of the shattered boat. I implore you, Captain Capstan, to steer your boat, so that, if such is the case, they may be picked up."

"It would be a hard matter, my dear girl," Capstan answered sadly, "to find the particular spot where the craft was stove. But Providence may reward our s'arch."

"And if it does," cried the professor of languages, "there will be another important item for my journal! Dear me! he was a good scholar, and I hope we may find him."

The captain arranged his sails so that he might keep off a point or two, and the cutter gathered headway upon her new course.

The search was continued for a couple of hours, but without success. Just as Capstan gave it up, the professor stated that he heard a faint cry off the weather-bow; but, as a large bird went rushing past the boat the next moment, Capstan concluded that Quill's eagerness to obtain items had so excited his imagination as to cause him to mistake the screaming of this creature for a human voice.

So the cutter was again put before the wind; and the men, leaning from their thwarts, spoke in low, sad voices of the fate of their shipmates. Little did they imagine that, at this very moment, the second mate was not much more than a quarter of a mile from their boat, clinging to one of the mast-poles of the launch.

CHAPTER V.

ADRIFT AND IN BONDS.

THE fate of the launch had been sealed by that last shot from the schooner. It struck the little craft on the bow, opening it and cutting away one of the small spars to which a sail was attached. The boat filled and sunk, leaving the men struggling in the water. Loring and Tom Pool, the only swimmers there, contrived to drag their two shipmates to the spar, to which they clung with a tenacious grasp. Soon, however, the schooner was seen bearing down upon them. Her rigging, her sails, and her bows, were alive with her dusky crew, who yelled and shouted with demoniacal triumph. Some of them were armed with muskets, some with pistols, and a few carried boarding-pikes.

"They are going to fire upon us first, and run us down afterward!" cried Tom Pool.

He was right; they did so.

Loring's three shipmates were killed; he was the only one of that unfortunate crew who rose to the surface after the vessel had run over them. He had saved himself by diving far down in the watery depths. He afterwards came up far astern of the schooner, and thus escaped observation. Very soon, the vessel dashed off in chase of the cutter, until, finally, she was screened from

Loring's view by the fog. He then swam to a spar and lashed himself to it by means of a rope that had been used as a sheet for one of the sails. At the moment when Capstan gave up the search, he had remained thus for two hours. The cutter had passed several times within a hundred and fifty yards of him, and yet he had known nothing of its vicinity, though, had the crew shouted, he might easily have heard them. His situation was sad enough. Alone upon the wide ocean, supported by a solitary spar, exhausted by his late exertions, feeling both hungry and thirsty, despairing of being picked up, he could only anticipate suffering and death. A presentiment that the cutter had escaped, that Grace Greenville was safe, cheered him, however, in the midst of his despair. He derived much pleasure, even now, from thinking of her. She had exerted a pleasing influence upon his spirit. While he lived, he could not forget the music of her voice, the light of her soft brown eyes.

The day wore on; the shadows of night gathered around him. He shouted long and loud, in the faint hope that some vessel might now be near. But he heard only the noise of the waves as they dashed together, and the screaming of the sea-bird as it whirled in circles over his head. He was so exhausted that he found it difficult to keep his eyes open. Once he fell into a doze, and had begun to dream that he was again on board of the Rainbow, when he was awakened by the splashing of a wave into his face. He rubbed his eyes, feeling a little confused; but the reality of his situation soon broke upon his mind. Still fast to the spar—still drifting along with the everlasting currents of the ocean.

He did not allow his eyes to close again.

A few hours after midnight, the fog having by this

time cleared, he saw the full moon emerge from a cloud
in the west.   A long, broad stream of light now lay like
a silver pathway athwart the surface of the ocean.
Shooting across it, far in the distance, a dark outline
greeted for an instant the vigilant eyes of the young
sailor.   He leaned eagerly forward, but the vision had
vanished.   Soon after, he saw it again ; it was nearer,
more distinct than before ; it was approaching.   At
length it glided into the floating pathway of silver, and
he uttered a cry of joy.   He could distinguish the flashing
of paddles, the outlines of human heads ; he could hear
voices chanting a strange, wild chorus.   Three times he
shouted with all his strength, but there came no response.
He unfastened the rope by which he was tied, and strad-
dling the spar, shouted again.   He was heard this time,
for a yell, a savage yell, that made him shudder, broke
upon his ears.   The paddles flew faster through the water ;
he was soon able to make out a long canoe filled with
half-naked figures ; later he could distinguish their faces,
disfigured by hideous marks of yellow and blue colours,
and crowned by great fiery masses of hair.   He knew,
by these signs, that the men were savages, belonging to
some one of the Pacific Islands.   They were soon near
enough to seize him, and they dragged him into the
canoe.   They stopped paddling, and, crowding up to him,
peered into his face, all talking together in a tongue unknown to him.   Calmly returning the glances of their
wild, fierce eyes, he strove to answer, by signs, the ques-
tions which he imagined they asked.   They paid no attention to his motions, however, but continued to screech
and jabber, apparently getting more angry with him every
moment, because he was unable to reply to them.   Their
eyes flashed upon him like coals of fire ; one of them

shook a great war-club in his face; another pointed a
spear at his heart. He thought it best to show an un-
daunted front, so he looked at them steadily, and though
his heart beat fast, yet there was no expression of fear in
his bronzed face. The savages were evidently on their
return from some warlike expedition. Their breasts and
arms were covered with contusions and scars; there was
a seriously wounded native lying near the bow of the
canoe; there were many broken spears and war-clubs
in the vessel. Loring coolly pointed to the prostrate
islander—to the damaged weapons—to the scarred bosoms
around him—and glanced inquiringly into the face of
the man nearest him. This person, he believed, was a
chief, for the others listened deferentially when he
spoke. He nodded with a sort of wild dignity upon
encountering the young sailor's expressive glance, and, as
though pleased with his cool behaviour, burst into a
laugh. Then pushing aside the threatening spear and
the uplifted club, he said something to his dusky crew,
who immediately sat down and commenced plying their
paddles. The chief took his station near the stern, and,
folding his arms over his broad bosom, kept his eyes fixed
upon the second mate. More than once the latter saw
the native's face betray a peculiar expression; he would
have given worlds to know what was passing through that
untutored mind. Glancing round him, he could not help
admiring the swiftness and regularity with which the
paddles were moved. The arms of the savages being long
and flexible, were peculiarly fitted for this work, while their
muscular but supple frames betokened their great
capacity for endurance. The only garment worn by each
was a piece of tappa (cloth)—probably bought from the
captain of some trading vessel—which, being secured

about the waist, hung a little below the knee. Their skin, of a dark olive tint, fairly shone with cocoa-nut oil, and their hair, which was coloured red, was arranged so as to look like great bunches of oakum. The length of the canoe was not less than forty feet; the number of its occupants thirty. Very soon they all broke forth into a wild chorus, similar to that which Loring had previously heard. Their voices were loud and clear, not altogether unmusical, and the second mate felt a throb of wild pleasure as he listened.

"If Professor Quill were only here," thought he, "what an item for his journal."

Day was now beginning to break, and land was visible ahead of the canoe. Soon the young sailor was able to distinguish the cocoa-nut trees upon the beach, and also a number of females standing near the water's edge. The chief rose and uttered a scream, so loud and shrill that it penetrated Loring's brain like a knife. The noise of the chorus was as different from this cry as is the clanging of cymbals from the wildest shriek of a Scottish bagpipe. In response, the women begun to dance about the beach, laughing, screaming, and clapping their hands. The canoe struck the sand soon after, and the natives sprung out, motioning to the young sailor to follow. He obeyed, and the next moment was completely hemmed in by the females, as they rushed from all sides to embrace the dusky warriors. The simultaneous cackling of twenty flocks of geese could scarcely have been heard in the din which followed. The young women screeched, laughed, and clapped their hands; the men, swinging their clubs around their heads, yelled like demons, while, strangely mingling with these joyful demonstrations, there rose, now and then, a howl of unearthly lamentation from an old withered crone, who knelt by the prostrate form of the wounded native. He was probably her son: his bleeding head was upon her knee; her long grey hair fell about his face.

Presently, the chief lifted his arm with a dignified motion, and said something to his warriors, upon which three of them lifted the sufferer and bore him off, followed by the old woman, still howling and moaning in a distracted manner. By this time, the tumult having in a measure subsided, Loring encountered the curious glances of the females. They gathered in front of him, peering into his face with their great black eyes, and now and then exchanging a word in a low voice. Some of them were quite pretty. Their faces were not painted, their features were good, their skin of an olive tint. Their hair, not being coloured, hung below their waists in black shining masses. They wore strings of beads around their necks, and green wreaths about their foreheads. In addition to the cloth secured about the waist, each was decorated with a pretty piece of red silk, worn gracefully upon the shoulders. As the silk was quite new, Loring concluded that some trading vessel from Japan had recently visited the island. An old man, who had lately joined the group, seemed to guess his thoughts by the expression of his eyes. He tapped him upon the shoulder and addressed him in broken English:—

"You, look-ee! much fine cloth. Ship come here t'ree week ago. Sell plenty silk for cocoa-nut and banana."

"I am both surprised and glad, my friend," exclaimed the captive, "to hear you speak my language. I feared that I should not be able to make myself understood by—"

"Oh, yes!" interrupted the old man, " me can talk white man tongue. White man long ago carry me away in ship. That's way learn speak English. White man beat, strike, kick much!" he added, with flashing eyes. "No like 'em for dat. Kill 'em all; best way to do."

Before the second mate could reply, the chief said something to the old man, who, bowing his head deferentially, turned again to the sailor.

"Onolo, de chief, say like to know how you come float on pole in de water."

Loring told his story in a few words, and the interpreter, in his turn, related it to Onolo, who then conducted the young man to a large hut, situated near a grove of coaco-nut trees and overlooking the sea. It evidently was the home of the chief, for, upon his entrance, an old woman flew to a corner and brought forth a curiously-formed wooden dish containing roasted fish, bread-fruit, bananas, and cocoa-nut sauce. He seated himself upon a mat, and she put the dish before him. Then he motioned to Loring to sit down and partake of the food, and to the interpreter, who was the only native that had followed them into the hut, to place himself on his left. Loring was not slow in accepting Onolo's invitation. Between him and the chief the dish was soon emptied; and, after Guy had refreshed himself with a few deep draughts of water, contained in an odd-looking vessel shaped like a gong, he looked about him for some comfortable spot on which to stretch himself for a nap. Observing a heap of cocoa-nut mats in one corner, he rose, and was moving towards them, when the chief, with a loud screech of displeasure, motioned to him to sit down again. He did so, at the same time requesting the interpreter to inform Onolo that he felt very tired and sleepy. This, however, the old man refused to do.

" You get sleep, plenty, pretty soon. Sleep so you no wake more," he said, with a hoarse laugh.

" Surely you don't mean that Onolo, after treating me in this kind manner, intends to have me killed ?"

" T'ink so. Hope so. Give plenty eat and drink to make fat. Know what me mean now ?"

The young man shuddered, but encountering at this moment the scrutinizing gaze of the chief, he even forced a smile.

" Do you know, my friend," said he, addressing the old man " that to kill, roast, and eat a poor sailor is a most un-civilized way of—"

" Ah ! me know what dat mean !" interrupted the native. " Dat mean savage. Well, me savage Mono, when white man take me 'way. White man—civilize, you call him—make me more savage. Kick, strike, knock poor Mono on de head. Me call dat more savage as islander."

Before Loring could reply, Onolo addressed a few words to the interpreter, who then rose and left the hut. He returned in a quarter of an hour, accompanied by three hideous-looking savages, whom the sailor was certain he had not seen before. Two were of gigantic stature, the other was short, with a tremendous breadth of chest and enormous head. They were armed with the war-club, each of which was so large and heavy, that the task of wielding it with effect might have been thought impossible by the young man but for the ease with which it was carried.

Onolo screeched forth a welcome, and the three visitors, scowling darkly at Guy, seated themselves on the

right of the chief. The old woman, who for some time
had remained in a distant corner, staring curiously at the
sailor, now moved to one side of the rude habitation and
brought forth four well-filled pipes, with large wooden
bowls and reed stems of enormous length. In the bowl
of each she put a burning coal procured from the
smouldering embers of a fire near the door of the hut;
then, with a reverential bend of her head, presented the
smoking treasures to Onolo and his three guests, who
received them with a simultaneous grunt of satisfaction.
They were soon puffing away and conversing together in
low, earnest tones. By the frequent glances directed
towards him, Loring knew that he was the subject of consultation. The short savage looked particularly vindictive,
nor was the expression upon the face of the other two
guests of a nature to reassure dim.

"What are they saying?" he ventured at length to
inquire of the interpreter. "Nothing very flattering to
me, I should judge."

"S-s-sh!" muttered the old man, in a low voice. "Dey
all great chiefs. Must no speak when dey speak!"

The consultation lasted until the pipes were smoked
out. Then Onolo said something to the short savage,
who thereupon sprung to his feet, threw himself
upon Loring, and, before the latter could make
any resistance, hurled him upon his back. His
huge muscular knee was upon the breast of the prostrate man in a moment, and his war-club lifted as
though to deal a fatal blow. Guy could not move, for
another savage had seized his arms, a third had grasped
his ankles. He was utterly powerless. The knee upon
his breast felt like some great iron weight; the grasp
upon his arms and ankles was like that of a vice. He

saw the head of the ponderous club quivering above him; he believed that in a moment it would descend, with crushing force, upon his skull.

Why did not the savage strike at once? What pleasure could he derive from torturing him in this manner? The cruel, exultant expression of the native's face inspired him with horror and indignation. His eyes flashed glances of defiance into those of his tormentor. Onolo—who, all this time, had been closely scrutinizing his countenance—suddenly uttered a grunt and a laugh of satisfaction. Then he spoke a few words, and Guy was released. He sprung to his feet, and, enraged beyond all bounds, would, the next moment, without thinking of consequences, have thrown himself upon the short savage, had not the interpreter and the chief grasped him by the shoulders.

"You very brave!" cried the old man. "Chief do dis for see whether you so. S'pose you said, ' No kill! no kill!' he kill quick. But you no dis, and so he say he keep you for one warrior for him. He say you make good warrior; so he no let 'nudder white man come and take you. Go sleep now, s'pose, you like."

The three guests having by this departed, Loring made his way to the mats, and, throwing himself upon them, dropped at once into a sound slumber.

CHAPTER VI.

LAND, HO! AND SOMETHING MORE.

THE cutter had been kept steadily upon her course for four hours, when Block uttered an exclamation, and pointed directly ahead.

"Ay, ay," cried Capstan, "there it is—the land. Cheer

up my dear girl," he added, turning to Grace, "we'll soon be ashore. Don't you see that headland looming up through the fog?"

She did see it, and tried to smile, though her heart beat heavily. She missed the cheery voice and manly form of Loring; she believed that he had perished—that he had sacrificed his life for her sake. The cloud upon her spirit, she thought, would never pass away.

Soon the boat's keel grated upon a sandy beach, and the men sprung ashore. Block, with great gallantry, helped the young girl out of the cutter.

"Your troubles have imperceptibly diminished," said he. "We are now on dry land, and it's probable that we'll inscribe a sail before long."

"Ay, ay!" cried Capstan, "this headland rising above us, is just the place for a good lookout. Cheer up, my dear girl!"

"Dear me, how delicious!" exclaimed the professor of languages. "Here we are on a lonely island! This is an adventure, indeed."

"Pull up your cutter, lads," continued the skipper, "and get it behind these two rocks alongside of us as soon as you can. It is best," he added in a whisper, to his mate, "to have it out of sight. I shouldn't wonder if we saw that infarnal schooner when the fog clears.

"Very likely," answered Block; "and for that same reason, we must direct our huts where they can't be seen. While the men are getting out the contentments of the cutter, I'll just go and reconsider the island, to find a good spot for us."

The captain consenting, Block set out upon his expedition. Passing the headland, he made his way through a small grove of cocoa-nut trees, and came suddenly upon a little valley watered by a clear stream. A better place, he thought, for the building of huts, could not have been found; so he returned and reported his success to the captain. Two of the men were sent to the valley to commence the work of erecting shelters. The rest soon followed, carrying boat-sails, mast-poles, kegs, packages of provisions, and many other articles taken from the cutter. Before night, the huts, two in number, and built of the branches of bread-fruit and cocoa-nut trees, were completed. One was very small, and situated about fifteen yards from the other, which was of larger dimensions. The first was designed for Grace—the last, for the occupation of the four men and two officers. Upon entering her "palace," the young girl was much pleased with the manner in which it was fitted up. That she might have a soft couch, the men had first covered the inclosed space of ground with a thick carpet of leaves plucked from one of the bread-fruit trees that skirted the edges of the valley, and afterward spread over this a couple of thick blankets. In one corner of the apartment lay the chair-cushions upon which she had reposed while in the cutter, and not far from these stood a breaker (a small cask), containing fresh water procured from the stream. Fastened to the vessel, by means of a piece of rope-yarn, was a tin cup, which had been scoured and polished until it shone like silver. This was the property of old Tom Rocket, who could never have forgiven himself had he left upon it a single spot of rust to soil the lips of such a "nice little lass" as Grace Greenville. Besides the conveniences already mentioned, the young girl was surprised to see a small looking-glass, together with a piece of candle and some matches, lying upon an empty box. These articles had been provided by Block.

"A looking-glass," he had said to Capstan, "is one of the most inexcusable necessities of woman. For that reason, do you see, I've put one in her hut, and have besides thrown in the contingencies for striking a light, in order that she may see her inflection in the mirror."

While Grace was still occupied in surveying her apartment, she heard the voice of the mate outside of the canvas screen which had been fitted over the entrance of the hut.

"Will you be so good, my dear lass, as to participate with the rude fare that I've previded? A little mastication of this combustible material will do you good!"

So saying, he pushed into the apartment a small pan, containing some roasted salt beef, a few pieces of cocoa-nut, and four sea-biscuits. A tin cup, filled with smoking hot coffee, was next introduced, and the mate then withdrew. By this time the shadows of night had begun to mingle with the fog, and the sailors were gathered near a small fire, eating their supper and talking over their late adventures. Capstan was fast asleep in the large hut, having finished his meal before his crew begun theirs. He had left orders with Block to station a guard of two men near the huts, to give warning in case of the appearance of savages, and the mate had chosen Professor Quill and Tom Rocket to stand the first watch. Accordingly, after their shipmates had retired, the two lookouts took their places upon a small hillock, just beyond the lower edge of the valley. At the expiration of two hours they were relieved, but, at four o'clock A.M., it was again their turn to watch. The day was beginning to break when the distant noise of a chorus of wild voices was borne to their ears. The fog having by this time cleared, they ran to the headland and looked around them. There was soon light enough to enable them to make a discovery which the darkness had hitherto prevented. Looming up on their right, they saw a large island, green with groves of cocoa-nut and bread-fruit trees, and miniature forests of banana plants. Ridges of high land rose above the tops of the trees, crowned with luxuriant verdure and partially veiled by their clouds of floating mist. Far below lay the long, winding beach, curving round a number of little bays, and covered with sand as white as the foam by which it was washed. On one side, the beach sloped down to a small strait, about a quarter of a mile in width, and which separated the small island occupied by the party from the larger one upon which the two men now gazed. This, compared with its neighbour, was a perfect paradise.

" My eyes ! who would have thought !" exclaimed Tom Rocket ;" and," he added, clutching the arm of his companion, "do you see that ?"

He pointed to a distant promontory, and glancing quickly toward it, the professor caught a glimpse of a long canoe, as it was disappearing round the point.

" It was full of savages ! " cried the old seaman. " I saw 'em and their paddles. It was them that we heard a-chanting the chorus ! "

Little did either of the two men imagine that the second mate was in that canoe !

They were on the point of turning for the purpose of making their way to the hut, when the keen eye of the old seaman suddenly became riveted upon an object—a mere speck dotting the sea—far away to the eastward. With a suspicious shake of the head, he pointed it out to the professor.

" It's a sail ! " he exclaimed, "and in my mind it's not a friendly one."

"Oh, dear me!" exclaimed Professor Quill. "You don't say so? You don't mean to—"

"I can only guess," interrupted Rocket; "but, as is very nat'ral to suppose, I think it's the schooner."

"Why, bless me! I hope not!"

They ran to the hut, and, rousing Capstan and Block, informed them of what they had seen and heard. The captain seized his spy-glass, and made his way to the headland. The sail was too far off, however, to be seen very distinctly, even with the aid of the instrument.

"I can't make her out," he said to Block, who was watching him earnestly; "but, whatever she is, it is sartin she is a-coming this way."

He shut up his glass, and waited a full half-hour before taking another survey. The sail was much nearer than before: he had not surveyed it a minute when he lowered the glass.

"It's her, Block, for sartain!—it's the schooner?"

"I thought so. Do you think they have any suspense of our being here."

"I don't doubt it. We must all keep out of sight. Here," he added, pointing to a small mound of earth close by, "is a sort of breast-work, which will hide me from the rascals. While I stay here and watch their manœuvres, you, Block, had better go back to the huts, and caution the men to keep out of sight. If they stay where they are, they can't be seen. Don't let 'em stir from the spot."

"Ay, ay," replied the mate, and departed.

Capstan had remained in his position for several hours, watching the schooner, which was approaching at the rate of eight knots, and was now little more than a league distant, when he felt a hand upon his arm.

He turned, expecting to see Block, but was much astonished upon beholding, instead, the face of an old savage, hideously painted, and lighted by a pair of fierce, sunken eyes. He sprung to his feet, expecting to be attacked, but the native smiled grimly, and, stepping back a couple of paces, folded his arms over his wrinkled bosom.

"You t'ink me kill? Not so—no come to kill—no got war-club—no got spear. Me you feleng (friend)."

"Where did you come from? who are you?"

"Name Mono. Me come from dat oder island, where me stan' on hill and see huts. See you, too. So come here in canoe. What vessel dat yonder?" he added, before Capstan could speak. "Seem to be comin' dis way."

In his surprise at the sudden appearance of the native, the skipper had forgotten his caution, and, having, as we have said, sprung to his feet, he had remained standing, so that the upper part of his body was fully exposed to the lookouts aboard the schooner. The last words of the savage now recalled him, as it were, to himself, and, as quick as a flash, he again crouched down behind the breastwork.

A peculiar expression beamed from Mono's hollow eyes.

"Seem much 'fraid of dat vessel. Got bad crew, s'pose?"

"Ay, ay, bad enough," answered the skipper, "and —and—there she goes, sure enough, up into the wind, with her topsail aback; and there goes a boat into the water!"

"Dem Malay!" cried the interpreter, as he watched the forms of the sailors descending into the boat. "Me

know by dem dress, by dem yell.   Dey bad fellows.
Quick cut t'roat, s'pose get hold of you.   And dere dey
come dis way," he continued, seeing the bow of the boat
pointed directly for the headland.

Capstan did not reply: a few rapid bounds carried him
to the valley.   He was followed by Mono, upon seeing
whom, the men, grasping their cutlasses, sprung to their
feet.   That he was the foremost of some party of savages
in pursuit of their captain, was their first thought.

The skipper undeceived them in a moment.

"Quick, my lads!" he exclaimed, "pick up whatever
articles you can lay your hands on at once, and follow
me.   The schooner's boat is coming; we must take to
the cutter again.   If we stay here, we shall be discovered
and attacked in the course of half an hour."

"Malay got plenty men—plenty oar!" cried Mono.
"S'pose you go in boat, you be catch, quick.   Me, your
feleng; got big canoe on oder beach.   Go get him, paddle
him here.   Take you in, hide you in big island, where
Malay no find you.   Malay no see de canoe when go
cross water: land hide him."

And without pausing to see whether or not the captain
consented, the native darted off, and disappeared.

"What do you say, Block?   Shall we accept that
fellow's offer?   He seems friendly."

"It seems to be our only alterative, Captain
Capstan."

"Well, then, the matter is decided."

Ten minutes after, the little party were gathered upon
the beach that bordered the strait, ready to embark in
the canoe, which the savage was now paddling toward
them.

Grace turned pale when the man was near enough

to enable her to distinguish his hideous features, and Block immediately set about the task of calming her fears.

"His looks are distressing, Miss Greenville," said he; "but appearances are sometimes very receptacle, you know. I think you'll find it so in the present case. He knows it's to his own advantage to be friendly, seeing as he and his brethren drive a shrewd, intermingling traffic with marchant vessels!"

"Oh, dear me!" cried Professor Quill, "he is quite a character, and will make quite a figure in my journal!"

Soon after, the canoe struck the beach, and the whole party took their places. There were a dozen paddles in the vessel, and four of them were soon doing good service in the hands of the seamen. The canoe flew swiftly over the waters of the strait, which, as Mono had said, was screened from the approaching boat of the Malays by the peculiar formation of the shores. In a short time the party were safely landed, and, motioning them to follow, the native commenced to thread a narrow, winding path leading between thick clumps of shrubbery, among which the banana plant, loaded with its "yellow treasures," frequently pleased the eye. The men plucked and ate the fruit as they pursued their way, and they were almost sorry when they entered a thick grove of bread-fruit trees, where the earth, though beautiful in a moist carpet of long waving grass and curious flowers, was yet devoid of the profitable plant which had afforded them so much enjoyment.

Leading them on a quarter of an hour longer, the native suddenly paused in front of a high rock, situated in a forest of coaco-nut trees, and half-hidden by clambering vines and thick masses of shrubbery. Pushing aside the interlacing branches and leaves of a couple of young, curiously-shaped trees, he now disclosed the entrance to a large cave. The interior space of ground was thickly strewn with leaves, and in one corner there were a few mats.

"Dere," said Mono, with a smile, "go in dere all my 'felengs,' and Malay no come to trouble. Plenty warrior—plenty spear and club on dis island. S'pose come? drive 'way quick. Glad to go back to schooner!"

"Really," said the professor of languages, as the party moved into the cave, "this is quite romantic!"

"It is sartainly encouraging to find ourselves in this comfortable diploma!" cried Block, rubbing his hands, "these islanders know what's good for 'em."

"I hope," said Capstan, "that our friend won't forget us."

"Oh, no—me no forget. Before many hour, come again, and bring plenty to eat—banana, cocoa-nut, and fish. You all right—no fear."

After he had gone, Capstan drew forth his spy-glass, and placed it under his arm.

"I am going, Block," he whispered, "to the top of the rock, to get another look at the schooner. If anything happens you can call me. Keep your eye on the men, and don't let 'em stir from this spot."

"Ay, ay, sir, my secretion **may** be relied upon," responded the mate, with a bow.

The skipper left the cave, and was soon on the summit of the rock, crouching behind a heap of dry brushwood. From this position he could see the schooner, lying with her topsail aback and her jibs hauled down. Her rigging and yards were alive with men looking toward the smaller island. Upon the latter, Capstan saw, quite distinctly, the figures of her boat's crew moving hither and thither : occasionally, too, he heard a yell of demoniac disappointment.

"Ay, ay," he muttered, "you may s'arch and s'arch until doomsday, but you'll find nothing there !"

Half an hour afterward the Malays, having examined every part of the island, were gathered upon the summit of the headland. Capstan concluded that they were holding a consultation.

"They don't like to give us up," he said, mentally. "The trick that I sarved one of their boat's crews has worked 'em up to a high pitch, and made 'em eager for revenge. They haven't done looking for us yet."

A moment later, he saw them returning to the schooner in their boat.

"Can it be possible that they have given us up," he muttered. "I can hardly believe it, and yet it would seem so, by the way that boat is steering."

Suddenly he pointed his glass in another direction. A canoe shooting out from behind one of the promontories of the larger island, and containing a single individual, was naturally calculated to attract his attention. The vessel was heading directly for the schooner, which its occupant seemed in a great hurry to reach. A sudden suspicion flashed across the mind of the skipper.

Who was the native in the canoe ?

The glass was not powerful enough to enable Capstan to distinguish his features, but his bowed figure was certainly not unlike that of Mono, the interpreter.

What business had he with the schooner ? Perhaps he only wished to bargain with its crew for tobacco and cloth. It was quite customary for the Pacific Islanders to do this ; to exchange the products of their fruitful soil for some of the many useful articles contained in the vessels that visited their wild shores. Nevertheless, Capstan could not rid himself of his suspicions. He had felt a presentiment of evil ever since the interpreter had proposed to conceal the party. Now he was almost con vinced that the savage intended to betray them !

He watched the canoe until it glided alongside of the schooner ; then he descended the rock, and entering the cave, communicated his fears, in a low voice, to his mate. Block was startled ; he had not for a moment doubted the faith of the interpreter. Even now he found it diffi- cult to believe that the man meditated treachery.

"I think you are mistaken, Captain Capstan, I—"

"Ay, ay," interrupted the skipper, "that's the way with you, Block. Woman, and woman only, is your 'forty.' Where man is consarned you are sure to fail in your reckoning."

"Perhaps you are right, Capstan : I think you are. Them that doubt my knowledge of woman, or my 'th'rough' versatility with the dictionary, must have a small decorum of brains ; but men—especially savages—'

"What do you think we had better do," the skipper again interrupted. "Shall we leave this, and seek another place of concealment ?"

"It's our only alterative," replied the mate ; " that is if you are certain that treachery is under commisera- tion."

At that moment the noise of approaching footsteps and savage voices was heard. Glancing through the small opening in the shrubbery, the party saw a number of dark forms apparently moving toward them. A minute after, they vanished, and supposing that they had turned off in another direction, Capstan whispered to his men to get down on their hands and knees, and creep cautiously out of the cave.

"Take the path to the right," he added, "I will follow with Miss Greenville."

The professor of languages was the first to emerge from the cave, but he had proceeded only a few paces, when a long spear whistled past his head and struck the side of the rock. The next moment there was a rush through the shrubbery, and a dozen armed savages appeared, yelling, screeching, and brandishing their clubs.

"Oh, dear me!" exclaimed Quill, as he quickly backed into the cave, "this is really too bad. I could have sworn that our escape was certain."

"What do you think now, Block?" inquired Capstan. "Those fellows were set to watch us. Doesn't that look like treachery?"

"It is sartingly a ' new-for-wrong!' answered the mate. "We are in an unembarrassed situation, and I don't see how we are to expatriate ourselves out of it."

The skipper remained silent : with a gloomy brow— with one arm thrown protectingly around the waist of the shrinking girl, he stood surveying the savages who had formed a line within a few yards of the rocky entrance. They were gesticulating and talking in an excited manner ; their eyes were directed toward the face of Quill, with an expression of wonder. Some one of them advanced and beckoned to him.

"Why, bless me!" he exclaimed. "What can it mean? What can this fellow want of me?"

He stepped boldly forward, and pausing in front of the native, looked him steadily in the face. The native grinned, and placed a finger upon each of the green glasses.

"Hookee—pooki—hee-hee!" he exclaimed, turning up the whites of his eyes.

"I don't understand you, my dear sir," replied the professor, "but if you mean that you want my glasses, I can assure you that you won't get them without a struggle. Oh, dear me—no!"

The native grasped the speaker's hand, and nodding his head toward his brother warriors, gently drew him from the cave. The professor offered no resistance, but, turning toward Grace, he remarked that he believed his spectacles would do her a good service, and advised her to keep up her spirits.

"What the deuce do you mean?" inquired the skipper.

"Simply that, by means of my glasses, I may be able to engage the attention of the natives, thus affording you all a chance to escape."

The skipper looked amazed, and, guessing his thoughts, Block nodded to him significantly.

"You'll never commit such a 'new-for-wrong' again, Captain Capstain," he exclaimed, "as that of accusing us men of l'arnin' of a want of courage. Them green spectacles will eventually remunerate us all."

Quill had now reached the line of savages. Grunting and screeching, these wild men gathered round him, closely scrutinizing the glasses, and tapping them with their fingers. But, when the professor pulled them from his eyes, the astonishment of the natives knew no bounds. All started back with cries of superstitious horror, except one, who had learned a few words of English from the interpreter. He stealthily advanced, and touched the eyelids of the professor with one of his thumbs, in a hesitating manner.

"Funny eye," he muttered, "one—two: take off

one eyes, oder eyes still dere. Dat queer; neber see before!"

"Why, it's the simplest thing in the world, my dear friend," replied Quill. "I was born that way. With my double eyes, I can see objects a hundred miles off! Oh! dear me—yes!"

So saying, he sat down, put the glasses upon the ground, and quietly folded his arms.

"Mudder hab two eyes dat same way?—and fader?" inquired the native, as he closely scrutinized, without daring to touch them. "Say—speak-ee me—was dat how come wid double eye?"

"Certainly, my dear sir—certainly."

"S'pose dese eyes you takee off break—what den?"

"They would snap a nerve and kill me at once—they would, really!"

The native's whole countenance was now twisted into such a ludicrous expression of wonder, that Quill could scarcely refrain from laughing. The wild youth communicated the startling "truths" he had learned to his brother warriors, who then advanced, and, stooping upon their hands and knees, began to scrutinize the wonderful glass eyes lying upon the ground. This was exactly what the professor desired: there was now an opportunity for the occupants of the cave to escape. Nor were they slow to take advantage of it. They cautiously glided from the cave, their feet making no noise upon the soft damp earth, and struck into a path bordered by thick clumps of shrubbery. The noise made by the brushing of their garments against the leaves and branches was unheard by the natives amid the tumult of their excited voices; and the party were soon many hundreds of yards from the rock.

" It is too bad," remarked Block, "to leave the professor in the hands of them delectable savages. Who knows what will become of him ?"

" He will contrive to escape, easily enough, I dare say," replied Capstan. " At any rate, while he's in possession of them glasses, he won't come to harm."

Grace looked up anxiously.

" I am afraid," said she, " that Mono has seen spectacles before now. You remember that he told us while we were in the canoe, that he had sailed in some ship, and had visited many foreign countries. Now, when he comes to hear of the miraculous story of the glasses, will he not punish our friend for imposing upon his brother warriors ?"

" Ay, ay, I didn't think of that," said Capstan. " I remember now that Quill's glasses didn't seem to surprise the savage you speak of when he was with us. However, the professor is shrewd, and I doubt not will contrive to escape before Mono is encountered. I was sorry to leave him, but we had no other alternative. Hark, here they come !" he added, as a succession of yells, followed by the loud rustling of the shrubbery behind them, saluted the ears of the party. " This way, men—this way !"

So saying, he plunged among the bushes that skirted the path, drawing Grace after him. He continued his way for a few yards, then crouched to the ground, the young girl following his example. Block and the rest of the party did the same. In this position they remained, until they had seen the tops of the natives' spears go past them; the savages supposing that the fugitives were ahead. Then rising, they continued forcing their way through the shrubbery, until they found themselves in a deep valley, containing a number of rocks, and shadowed by overarching branches of trees. Here they paused in order that the young girl might rest herself, though she declared that she yet had strength enough remaining to go much further. There was a small stream in the valley, and from this Tom Rocket brought her a cup of cool water, with which she bathed her forehead and temples.

" I'm afraid we'll have a preponderous time in getting the lass out of the present calamitous position," Block remarked in a whisper to Capstan, " though she's a true woman—one of the Mrs. Blocks all over—and bears everything without a rumour."

"Ay, ay," replied Capstan, " and—hark ! what is that ?"

Every man sprung to his feet : a rustling noise was heard among the bushes that skirted one side of the valley. The next moment the curved nose of Professor Quill, again bridged by his green spectacles, was thrust over the top of a clump of shrubbery.

" Why, dear me ! So you are here !" he said, as he advanced. " I am so glad they didn't overtake you."

" We owe you many thanks !" cried Grace, impulsively.

" Ay, ay, so we do !" exclaimed Capstan. " You are a brave man, after all, professor."

" Well, I'm not quite a coward, I believe," answered Quill, " and I'm not quarrelsome either."

" And yet, I'd judge you'd been a-dealin' blows, my lad, by the looks of your sleeve," cried Tom Rocket, " seeing as there's spots of blood upon it."

" Why, bless me, yes ! So there are !" cried Quill. " The truth is that the savages, when they saw you were gone, left one of their number to guard me, while the rest started off in pursuit. We were quite sociable over the spectacles—my companion and I—until it suddenly struck me that I might make my escape. So away I went, but the native being the best runner, soon overtook me, and aimed a blow at my head with his club. This I dodged, and then ran him through with my cutlass—that was all, really. Afterward, I dashed off through the shrubbery, taking a direction which, I am glad to perceive, has led me here."

"Well, well," said Capstan, "I don't know, after all, as l'arning does make cowards of all, but—"

"There was never a greater 'new-for-wrong' in the world than that idea!" interrupted Block, "it's a gilded conscience, not l'arning, that makes cowards."

CHAPTER VII.

LOKO! LOKO! LOKO!

"I BELIEVE you are right," said Capstan, "after all. And now," he added, "we will continue our way, and try if we can't find some better hiding-place than is afforded by this valley. The natives will be sure to look for us here before long."

Accordingly, the party rose from the rock upon which they had been sitting, and striking into a narrow path that led through a miniature grove of banana plants, moved on in single file, Grace occupying the centre, between Block and Capstan. They had not gone far, when they saw smoke rising above the tops of a thick mass of bread-fruit trees, about a hundred yards ahead. The foremost man stopped, and turning, motioned to the rest to halt.

"I see a cluster of huts," he whispered, "and men, women, and children."

"We must try another direction, then," said the skipper. "We will file to the right."

They did so, and after they had pursued their new course for a mile, they found themselves in another valley. Its sides were thickly covered with brushwood, which, in some places, almost concealed the entrances to the caves and hollows among a confused pile of rocks.

"We will go no further, Block," said Capstan, halting the party. "If I mistake not we're now close upon the beach that borders the strait. Here we'll hide ourselves until night, when we'll make for the beach, from which I shall send you and the men to the other island to see whether or not the cutter is safe and sound. If it is, you shall launch it, and bring it to the beach, where Grace and I will be awaiting for you."

"An excellent idea!" cried Block, "if we can once get hold of the cutter again, we may contrive easily enough to preclude the vigilance of our enemies and get away."

So saying, he followed the rest of the party into a cave in one of the rocks. The skipper, with the assistance of his mate, contrived to arrange a mass of brushwood in such a manner that, while it concealed the entrance to their retreat, it yet admitted light enough to enable them to see each other's faces. One of the men, who, while among the banana plants, had filled a large canvas bag with the fruit, now poured the "golden treasures" upon the ground. Of these the party made a hearty meal, afterward regaling themselves with the milk of the cocoa-nut. They heard nothing to cause alarm until many hours had passed, when a sudden rustling in the shrubbery near the cave made them all start. Peering through small openings in the artificial screen, Capstan beheld the hideous face of a savage within a few yards of him. The native kept turning his eyes from side to side in an eager, suspicious manner, as though he felt convinced that the fugitives were not far off. Very soon, all were startled upon seeing the piercing orbs of the islander become fixed with a searching gaze upon the small twigs and branches by which they were concealed. Grace felt her heart beat loud and fast : it seemed to her that the man must see them now. There he stood, bending eagerly forward with his long spear in one hand and a heavy club in the other. He was tall and athletic, with shoulders of herculean breadth, and very long arms. His face, painted and covered with scars, was more hideous than any she had yet seen. She was, therefore, much relieved when the native, after continuing his survey several minutes longer, turned round and walked off quite leisurely, as though he had seen nothing to excite his suspicions.

"A narrow escape that," whispered Block. "I thought we would sartainly be individualized by that lubber's imperceptible glances."

"I am not so sartain that he did not discover us !" said Capstan, uneasily. "P'r'aps he knows we are here, and has gone off to inform some of his brethren."

"Oh, dear me! yes," said the professor, "that is quite likely, for, of course, he would not have ventured to attack us alone."

"In that case, the sooner we leave this place the better," responded the skipper. "It is nearly twilight already, and we'll soon be a-having the night shadows to help us."

"Suppose I go to reconsider," said the mate. "I

think that would be the best way before we venture to quit our retreat."

Capstan consenting, Block cautiously crawled out of the cave. He made his way to the foot of a cocoanut-tree that rose from a small open space of ground beyond the valley. Then, carefully looking round him to make sure that none of his enemies were in his vicinity, he threw off his shoes and climbed the tree. He was soon upon one of the topmost branches, a position that afforded him a good view of the island and the open sea. He was pleased upon discovering that the strait was only a quarter of a mile off.

" That's a highly entertaining sarcumstance," he muttered, " but, ' misfortunately,' there isn't a single canoe upon the beach. When we go for the cutter, we'll have to swim across that bit of water, and—"

He paused upon seeing a group of Malays and savages suddenly make their appearance upon the summit of a small ridge of land, a little to the left of the beach, headed by a native, whose figure certainly bore a striking resemblance to the one which had alarmed the party in the cave. The dusky band were not more than a quarter of a mile off and ·were rapidly approaching. Block felt that there was not a moment to lose. He quickly descended the tree, and, hurrying to the cave, made known his discovery. The party were ready to leave in an instant. Quitting their retreat, they cautiously but swiftly glided through the shrubbery, and, pursuing a course that carried them far to the rear of their enemies, they succeeded in gaining the beach by nightfall. The darkness was intense, with the exception of a gleam of silvery light in the eastern horizon, where the upper edge of the moon's disc had just become visible.

" Quick, Block! quick, my lads!" said Capstan. " Now is the time—before the moon rises—to go for the cutter. You can all swim, I believe."

" Ay, ay, sir," was the response, and shoes and jackets were thrown to the ground.

The men were soon in the water, headed by Block. The faint outlines of their heads disappeared a few minutes after from the gaze of the captain and his fair companion. But by the time they had gained the middle of the strait, a long broad stream of light from the rising orb, revealed them to the two spectators. The latter now fairly held their breath with suspense. By looking from any of the high ridges of land in the interior of the isle, the natives might easily have seen those dark heads moving through the waves. Soon, however, the beach was gained, and, creeping upon their hands and knees, the men disappeared around the base of the headland.

" They will soon have the cutter," whispered Capstan; " that is, provided them rascals didn't discover and destroy it, while they were on the island. Once in the boat, my dear girl, we'll at least have a better chance than we have now."

" But will the Malays not pursue us in their boats the same as before?"

" I think not at present. They've probably sent ashore the greater part of their men, and before they can get ready to follow us, we'll have the start of them by a league."

" Oh, I am glad to hear that!" she said, trying to seem pleased, "and—hark," she suddenly interrupted, laying a trembling hand upon his arm, " did you hear that?"

" No—what ? "

" The cracking of a branch ! It has stopped now."

They listened attentively for a repetition of the noise, and ere long it was again heard—this time more distinctly than before.

" There are several persons," he said ; " I know that by the noise that is made. I will go a little way to reconnoitre."

" No—no—not for the world, my friend—you—"

" Be not alarmed—stay here. I'll soon come back. It is important I should find out the direction they're going, so as to know whether or not to quit this position."

Though much alarmed, yet she offered no further objection, knowing that it would prove useless. He left her, creeping cautiously upon his hands and knees through a narrow archway formed by the interlacing of branches and vines above a crooked and narrow path. In a few moments he was lost to her view. With clasped hands and an anxious countenance, she bent forward and peered into the gloom. Suddenly she heard the sharp report of firearms, quickly followed by a wild cry. A moment later, a figure came staggering toward her. It was soon so near that she recognised Capstan.

" Fly !" he gasped hoarsely, and fell at her feet in the agonies of death.

Then she heard a yell, followed by the rushing of many footsteps. She threw a farewell glance upon the blood-stained brow of her wounded protector, staggered a few yards, and then, half-fainting, crawled amid the shrubbery that lined the bank. Luckily the sand was too dry and hard to take the impression of her slender feet, otherwise the party of savages and Malays, who now emerged upon the beach, must have tracked her at once. As it was, they passed so close to her hiding-place, that she might easily have touched one of them with her hand. They returned a moment later, and very soon she heard a noise that made her shudder. It was the splash of the dead body as it was thrown into the water. Not long afterward, she heard the party move into the shrubbery: through little openings among the twigs and leaves, she saw them crouch to the ground, with their backs turned toward her. Their low voices then broke upon her ear: a startling suspicion flashed into her mind. These men having seen the swimmers, and guessed their intentions, were lurking in ambush in order to attack them when they should return.

She must prevent this, if possible !

Cautiously emerging from her place of concealment, she glided rapidly along, upon her hands and knees, keeping in the shadow of the bank. She continued her way until an abrupt curve afforded her a position from which she could watch for the appearance of her friends without being seen by her enemies. Plucking a scarf from her shoulders, the brave girl stood ready to motion the seamen back the moment they should greet her vigilant gaze. But, while still watching the opposite beach with painful anxiety, she heard behind her, the noise of advancing footsteps ; together with that of a chorus of savage voices.

"Loko ! Loko ! Loko !"

The word was shrieked forth with startling vehemence: it rose distinctly above the crashing of shrubbery and the trampling of feet. She turned and crouched to the sand, her terror depriving her of the strength to move. A moment later, a tall, half-naked figure, with a hideously-painted face, came bounding over the top of the bank.

She uttered a faint cry and became unconscious. A loud exclamation broke from the islander: he stooped, lifted her in his arms with wonderful ease, and bore her to the edge of the sea, where, half concealed by a flat rock, lay a canoe large enough to contain three persons. This he launched with one hand, then placing the senseless form in the vessel, sprung in himself and paddled swiftly away from the shore. He had not proceeded more than a hundred yards, when a dozen fierce savages rushed over the top of the bank and bounded to the beach. Yelling, screaming, and gesticulating, they stood gazing toward the receding canoe. The name previously heard was shrieked forth again and again.

"Loko! Loko! Loko!"

But Loko did not seem to heed them. He continued to ply his paddles with the same vigour as before, and soon, to the eyes of the spectators, the canoe looked like a mere chip. Then its occupant, for the first time since quitting the beach, stopped paddling, and seemed to gaze with much interest upon the pale face of the senseless girl. Scooping up some water in the hollow of his hand, he bathed her forehead, her temples, and her long bright hair. But, while thus occupied, he suddenly heard the loud rushing of water upon his right. He turned and saw the schooner dashing swiftly along toward him. She was already but a hundred yards from the canoe. He seized his padddle and turned the head of his light vessel away from the approaching craft, as though intending to make an effort to escape. Then, as if aware of the uselessness of such an attempt, he dashed down the implement and quietly watched the schooner as she came on. She was soon within a few fathoms; her topsail was backed, and she luffed up into the wind. Then the fair smooth face of a youth of twenty was thrust over the quarter-rail.

"Who are you? What are you doing here?" he exclaimed. "Come aboard at once, or I'll blow you to pieces!"

The islander directed the canoe alongside: a Malay threw him a rope, and he fastened it to the light craft The dark faces of five of the pirates now appeared at the rail, and looking up, Loko encountered their fierce glances directed toward himself and his fair companion. She had by this time recovered her senses.

"How came I here?" she said, rising to her knees and glancing round her in a bewildered manner.

She saw the island far behind her; the remembrance of past events rushed suddenly upon her mind. With half-shrinking eyes she studied the hideous countenance of her companion, whom she soon recognised as the same islander she had seen on top of the bank. From him, her glances wandered to the schooner, to the dark faces peering over the rail, and, uttering a cry of terror, she hid her face with her hands. Loko inclined his head toward her as though about to speak, but before he could do so, the bight of a rope was thrown over him, and he was jerked unceremoniously to the deck. Then a Malay sprung into the canoe, and, lifting Grace from her feet, passed her to his shipmates, who drew her quickly over the rail. A moment later, the prisoners were surrounded by the five pirates, whose bloodshot eyes and unsteady heads proclaimed that they had been drinking deeply. Grace was so terrified that she could scarcely stand, but the islander returned the fierce glances of the pirates with a steady unflinching gaze. Soon the youth who had hailed the canoe made his appearance. Motioning the other seamen back, he eyed the two prisoners attentively. The light of the moon falling full upon him, revealed a countenance almost as smooth and delicate as that of a girl. There was, notwithstanding, an expression of cruelty in his brilliant black eyes, and his thin compressed lips, that alarmed the missionary's daughter much more than did the frowns and fierce ejaculations of the Malays. He wore a red cloth cap, with a yellow tassel, a pair of dark blue pants, and a white shirt.

" Can you speak English ?" he inquired abruptly of the islander, after he had surveyed him for some time.

" Little ; not too much," answered Loko.

" You are one of the natives of yonder island, are you not ?"

" Dat so—me belong dere."

" And why did you leave it in the way you've done ? Where were you going with this girl ?"

" Me see girl lying on beach—faint away. T'ink good time to carry off, and—and—make wife. Carry to some island far away, where oders no find me."

" She is one of those who escaped from the merchant ship, is she not ?"

" Me t'ink so."

" And don't you know that I made, this morning, a bargain with one of your painted brethren. He agreed to deliver into my hands the boat's crew, which he had hidden somewhere on the island, in exchange for so much cloth and tobacco. I immediately sent ashore all my men, with the exception of five you see before you, and the helmsman, to bring that crew to the schooner. They have been absent a long time, and—"

" Yes—yes !" interrupted Loko, " all dat me know. Interpreter speak me 'bout de bargain he make with you.

Reason crew no come back me t'ink is, 'cause white man get away from where he been put, and hide where no find him yet."

" And in the meantime you find this girl, who is one of those we are after, and try to cheat us out of her by carrying her off yourself !" cried the young captain, fiercely.

" No t'ink you want girl," replied Loko, " t'ink want men—dat all. S'pose me know you want girl, me bring quick."

" I have a mind to string you up to the yard-arm !" continued the captain. " If I thought you really intended to swindle me out of the girl, I would do so at once."

" Oh ! no, me honest—me no want to do that, T'ink you good man ; got plenty cloth and tobacco !"

" Well, then, jump into your canoe, and go back to the island as fast as you can. I will not harm you at present. But look out how you meddle with my affairs in future."

" Me no care go back to island," replied Loko ; " been sailor in ship once—same ship wid Interpreter ;—like to be sailor again : will sail in dis schooner, if you like.

The captain eyed the speaker keenly, from head to foot. He was tall, broad-shouldered, and active, and having been a sailor before, there was no reason why he should not be accepted.

" It's all right," said the young man, after a moment's reflection, " I will take you. But understand," he added, while a fierce gleam shot from his black eyes, " you must obey all my orders promptly, or you are a dead man !"

" Oh ! yes, yes, me understand," Loko coolly replied ; " nebber you fear. Me know my business."

"I will soon decide that point," replied the captain. "Do you see that jib?"

"Ay, ay, he been hauled down," promptly answered the islander, looking toward the boom.

"Well," continued the youth, drawing forth a gold watch, "lay out there and furl it. If it isn't stowed in five minutes, I shall hang you."

Loko smiled, but did not move.

"Did you hear me?" cried the pirate, fiercely, "in five minutes, or you're a dead man."

"Dere no hurry," quietly answered the islander. "Me can furl in one—two—t'ree minutes. Nebber take five."

"We shall see," responded the captain. "Take your own time if you choose. I have no objection to seeing you hung."

Loko seated himself on the fore-hatch, and drawing a wooden pipe and a match from beneath the cloth about his waist, was soon enjoying a quiet smoke. The captain's eye was fixed steadily upon his watch; a minute and a-half had already passed since he issued his order. A few seconds after, Loko rose, darted out upon the boom, and with wonderful activity commenced to gather up the sail. In two minutes, he had finished his task; the sail had never before been so neatly furled. A murmur of astonishment broke from the Malays; even the Captain looked surprised.

"You are a smart blueskin!" cried the youth, "and if you prove as expert with the cutlass as you are in handling canvas, I think I shall promote you."

Then directing at Grace a glance that made her shudder, he bade her follow him to the cabin. He extended his hand as he spoke, but she shrunk back, pale and trembling.

"Come!" he cried, laughing, "don't be afraid. A pretty way, this, to treat your future husband. I have never had a wife, but should like one, by way of variety."

"For heaven's sake," faltered Grace, moving quickly toward the rail, "let me leave this vessel! I—"

"No, no!" interrupted the captain, "that must never be. I cannot let my bird fly after I have caught it!"

He threw himself between her and the rail, and seizing one of her arms, ordered a Malay to grasp the other. Before the man could obey, Loko quickly advanced and took hold of her disengaged arm. The girl struggled vainly to release herself; she was hurried aft to the companionway and into the cabin. At the foot of the staircase, however, the islander let go of her arm, and breaking suddenly from the pirate, she bounded up the steps and was on deck in an instant.

"Why did you let go of her?" exclaimed the captain, directing, as he sprung toward the companionway, a fierce glance upon the islander. Loko darted forward, struck the speaker heavily upon the temple with his clenched fist. and, as the youth fell senseless at his feet, rushed upon deck. He found Grace struggling in the grasp of the helmsman, who had seized her to prevent her from jumping overboard. The brute had caught hold of her long hair, and was dragging her toward the cabin. The rest of the Malays, taking advantage of the captain's absence, had gone into the forecastle before the young girl reappeared on deck. Springing upon the wretch, the islander knocked him down with a blow of his fist, and assisted the maiden to rise. The man jumped to his feet, however, and picking up a wooden belaying-pin, hurled it at Loko's head. The pin, missing its destination, struck Grace near the temple, and she dropped senseless into the arms of the islander. Seeing him thus burdened, the pirate drew a knife, and rushed toward him. But, stepping quickly backward, he laid the girl upon the main-hatch, and seizing a crow-bar lying near him, dealt his antagonist a blow that felled him to the deck. The noise made by the men in the forecastle—for they were shouting and singing hilariously—had drowned that of the brief conflict outside, so that the islander was now enabled to make his way to the canoe and put his burden therein without being discovered. He was soon paddling swiftly away from the schooner in the direction of a sail which was faintly distinguishable in the moonlight, far away to the eastward. Occasionally, he would throw an anxious glance upon the pale face of the senseless girl, and when he had left the schooner a league behind him, he stopped paddling, and, in the same manner as he had done before, strove to restore his fair charge to her senses. While thus engaged, he fancied that he heard the sound of oars. Turning his eyes in the direction of the noise, he saw two boats speeding swiftly along, apparently in chase of him. The foremost of the two vessels was less than a league from the canoe, and the other about the same distance astern of the leading boat. They had hitherto been screened from his view by the schooner, which, having no man at the helm, had now swung off a couple of points. With an exclamation of surprise, the islander seized his paddle, and, fixing his eyes upon the distant sail which was evidently approaching, he urged his light vessel through the water with great rapidity.

CHAPTER VIII.

THE TRIPLE RACE.

BLOCK and his little party succeeded in gaining the rocks where the cutter had been concealed. They found the boat lying exactly as they had left it, and, at length, after working pretty hard, contrived to launch it.

" There !" cried the mate, as the boat splashed in the water, " that difficulty is exterminated at last. Jump in, my lads, and let us no longer refrain from gaining the spot where we left our two friends !"

The men sprung to their thwarts, and promptly seizing their oars soon pulled the vessel into the strait.

" Now, then," said Block, as he directed the cutter toward the spot where he had left Grace and the captain, " everything impends upon your exertions. The moon shines brightly ; there's every prospectus of our being seen. So pull like thunderbolts, my lads."

The men laid back to their oars with a will, and in a short time the boat was within twenty yards of the beach. Then the mate suddenly sprung to his feet and ordered the crew to stop pulling. They did so, and leaning forward Block carefully scrutinised the beach and the shrubbery lining the bank.

" I may have been mistaken," he whispered, " but I thought I disentangled the point of a spear, intruded for an instant above the top of them bushes."

" Oh, dear me !" ejaculated the professor, turning his green spectacles toward the shore, " I hope not. I have items enough for my journal already."

" I am sure I saw it," continued the mate, in a musing tone, " and what is still more auspicious, I haven't yet seen the forms of either Capstan or the girl. The figure of the skipper, as you all know," he added, raising his voice, "is plump enough to be popular. I don't think a cautious reconsidering would be out of place."

"I will go," promptly answered Quill. "I pride myself upon being a good swimmer."

"All right, professor, you may go. But be careful not to protrude yourself heedlessly into danger."

The professor dropped over the gunwale into the water, and swam toward the beach. He was soon upon the shore, so that the party concealed in the shrubbery had a plain view of his person. One of them, a Malay, aimed a pistol at his heart, and would have fired, had not the Interpreter, who was seated near him, grasped his arm.

"S'pose you fire, den oders go away. Best not fire, best not give 'larm; den all come 'shore!" he whispered.

Just then the professor started and stooping, closely examined a dark red stain upon the sand at his feet.

"Oh, dear me!" he muttered, after he had surveyed it for a few minutes, "that is blood, or I am much mistaken."

He turned away and commenced peering into the shrubbery, every moment expecting to behold the dead bodies of Capstan and the young girl. Soon he was so near the spot where the party were concealed, that the man nearest to the edge of the bank might have touched him by stretching out his hand. A moment later, he saw them; encountered the gleam of their fierce eyeballs, looking in the darkness of their retreat like those of tigers when prepared for a spring. With a single bound he cleared the strip of beach and plunged into the water just in time to escape a bullet and the point of a whistling spear.

The next moment, a dozen dark figures sprang from

the shrubbery and dashed after him. But, swimming rapidly under water, he contrived to gain the boat while his pursuers were yet five or six yards behind him.

"Now, then, lads!" cried Block, in a shrill voice, "let us see what you are comprised of. Pull, pull, every man, like thunderbolts!"

The crew cheered, each man whirled his oar through the water with the rapidity of a mill-wheel, and the boat flew like a discharged arrow toward the open sea.

Soon the dusky swimmers returned to the beach, and, after they had fired a few useless shots, they were seen running swiftly along the shore.

"Ay, ay, there they go, after their boat, I'm thinking!" cried the mate, "they'll soon be at our heels!"

"And yonder," said Tom Rocket, throwing a glance over his shoulder, "lies the schooner with her topsail aback. We mustn't go too close to her!"

"It's my opinion that she now hasn't men enough aboard of her to man a boat to pursue us. I don't think I can ever feel light-hearted again, lads," he continued, with a sigh; "for its very improvident now that Capstan and the girl have been murdered. That stain of blood in the sand proves it!"

"Why, bless me!" cried the professor, "it's enough to make us all heavy-hearted. The unhappy fate of the young girl and the skipper will make a sad item for my journal."

While the crew were thus expressing their sorrow, Block suddenly rose, and gazed long and steadily toward the eastern seaboard.

"Ay, ay," he exclaimed at last, "I thought so! it's a sail!" I've been a-looking at it for the last ten minutes, thinking it was a sea-bird."

" That's good news ! " cried Tom Rocket, " but it would seem much more joyful like if we had the girl and Capstan among us. It's been a sad business the loss of them, even though they've gone to the ' Elysian Fields !'"

" Ay, ay," cried Block ; " and though they say that Providence does everything for the best, I can't help a-thinking that this is a decisive ' new-for-wrong.' "

" P'r'aps, if they hadn't died in the way they seem to have done, hows'ever," said Tom, " they might have died in one which was all the harder ! They've gone to the thrones of heaven, which I'm told is of solid gold. Them's the blessin's of Christianity."

" Really," said Block, " you will permit me to observe that you take a highly indispensable view of the subject. Them that goes to heaven fairly rolls in the wealth of righteous principalities, which is far superior to gold. Them's the expectations of the humble, which has led a pure and superstitious life ! "

Just as he concluded, the Malay's boat was seen shooting from behind the promontory that projected from one end of the island. The crew of the cutter could hear the shouts and yells of the pirates as they strained at their oars. Having a good start of them, however, the fugitives doubted not that they would succeed in reaching the sail ahead in time to escape their pursuers. Soon, while passing astern of the schooner, they heard an exclamation of surprise from Block. About a league ahead, he saw the outline of the canoe occupied by Loko and his senseless companion. Although the head and shoulders of the islander were visible, the girl, of course, could not be seen, as she was lying in the bottom of the vessel.

" Ay, ay, I'll be swung up ! " exclaimed the mate, " if I don't think it's him—that same reconsidering rascal who was spying about the 'Rainbow.' He is now paddling off to find out the character of that sail ahead of him, or I'm much mistaken!"

"Dear me!" cried the professor. "I hope he'll catch a Tartar!"

"So do I; but, in the meantime, them impenetrable rascals are fast gaining on us. Don't slacken up any, my lads!"

The crew strained every muscle. Their breath came forth in short quick gasps; their arms ached with their labour. It was a hard task for only four men, that of urging the heavy boat so swiftly through the water. And in spite of their almost superhuman exertions, their pursuers continued to gain upon them. The boats were now less than two hundred yards apart. Suddenly, the schooner was also seen to join in the chase. On she came, scooping up the water with her graceful bows, and rapidly lessening the distance between her and the boats. Block's countenance fell; escape now seemed impossible. The sail ahead, though approaching, was yet more than a league distant; while the schooner was but half that distance astern of the fugitives.

"We are sartainly in an indispensable position!" exclaimed the mate. "Be ready, lads, to jump up, cutlass in hand, when I give the word. The boat will soon be upon us, and we must sell our lives as dearly as we can; though we may be run down by the schooner before it comes to that."

"Dear me!" cried Professor Quill, "can it be possible that I am not to live to see my journal published, after all? I am afraid that will be the case—I am, really."

"Ay, ay, it'll be up with us all, I'm thinkin," said Tom Rocket, "and all of us that's done our duty will go,

I hope, to the ' Elysian Fields !' There's the other boat now, not more than a hundred and fifty yards from us !"

Five minutes after, the schooner passed the pursuing boat.

" Cut 'em down, lads ! Show 'em no mercy !" shouted the musical voice of the captain as his vessel dashed swiftly on.

Block heard these words, and also the exultant cries of the Malays, in response.

He turned to his crew with a grim smile.

" We won't be run down, my men, after all. The schooner will leave us to be taken care of by the boat. So we'll have a chance at least to fight a little before we are cut up."

" Bless me ! that's encouraging !" cried the professor of languages ; and he quietly cocked his smoking-cap on one side of his head, to make himself look nice.

On came the schooner, sweeping over the sea like a bird. She passed the fugitives' boat without offering to molest it. She was evidently in pursuit of the canoe, which was now less than a league ahead of her. The islander, with his eyes bent alternately upon the approaching sail, and the boats, and the schooner astern, continued to ply his paddle with the same energy as before. The young girl was still unconscious, the light of the moon fell softly upon her pale cheeks, her drooping eyelashes, and bright brown hair. The schooner, continuing upon its course, was soon so near the canoe, that those on board could see the prostrate form of the unconscious girl. A moment after, a faint tinge of colour suffused her cheeks, her lips parted, she opened her eyes. Loko turned toward her ; he encountered her bewildered gaze, as she rose, and was about to speak to her, when the sharp crack of a musket came from the vessel in chase, and pressing his hand upon his side, the islander fell to the bottom of the canoe. With a low cry, the young girl bent over him, looking down upon his upturned face. The blood was flowing from a wound just above his right hip; she believed that he was dying. He smiled faintly, and tried to speak, but only a faint murmur came from his lips.

The next moment, Grace heard the dull booming of a heavy gun, then the howling of a shot over her head, followed by a loud crash behind her, and turning, she saw the shattered jib-boom of the schooner drop into the sea. The vessel tacked at once, and stood off, hoisting the recall signal for her boat. This was now within twenty yards of the cutter; and, firing a farewell volley at the fugitives, its occupants, with a yell of disappointment, began to pull for their vessel. They were soon aboard, and the boat was then hoisted up.

"Three cheers, my lads!" cried Block, turning toward his crew, not one of whom had been injured by the shots of the pirates; "three cheers! The schooner is showing her heels! Our preservation is identified!"

Off went the hats of the crew, and the cheers were heartily given—the professor in his excitement, throwing his smoking-cap into the sea.

"That was a pretty shot," cried Tom Rocket, as the men again seized their oars. "It took off the schooner's boom as neatly as a whistle. There's no doubt, now that yonder fellow"—pointing toward the approaching craft—"is a sloop-of-war. I thought so, from the first."

"Ay, ay," responded Block, "and I shall sartainly feel surprised if the pirate escapes her. Why, my eyes!" he added, bending eagerly forward, "if there isn't a figure that looks ostensibly like that of a female a-sitting in the canoe ahead of us."

All eyes were at once turned in the indicated direction.

"Dear me!" cried the professor, "it was a man a little while ago! it was, really!"

"Pull ahead! pull like thunderbolts!" cried Block, as a sudden suspicion flashed through his mind.

The men exerted themselves, and the cutter was soon within a foot of the canoe.

"Grace Greenville! I suspected so!" cried Block.

She sprung to her feet, and turned with a cry of surprise.

A moment later she was in the boat.

She pointed toward the prostrate figure of the islander in the canoe.

"He was wounded by a shot from the schooner!" she cried, and, remembering the prompt manner in which he had rescued her from the grasp of the Malay, she added, "He has been very friendly to me! For God's sake, let him be put in the boat, and carried as speedily as possible to the vessel which is approaching us."

"Why, bless me—how strange!" exclaimed Professor Quill; "another item for my journal."

"I wouldn't have believed that one of them savages had a sparkle of humanity in his bosom!" cried Block, "if I hadn't heard it from Miss Greenville's own lips! Put him in the boat, lads!"

This was done, and a bright gleam lighted for a moment the dim eyes of the sufferer, as he encountered the glances of the boat's crew.

"Pull ahead!" was ordered, and the oar-blades splashed in the water.

Explanations then ensued between Grace and the mate.

E

Block was much pained upon learning the particulars of Capstan's death, for he had secretly nourished a faint hope that his old chum had only been wounded, and had crawled to some hiding-place where he might eventually be discovered by the sloop-of-war. This vessel being now only half a league from the boat, the latter was soon alongside. Steps were lowered from the gangway for the accommodation of the young girl, and a bluff-looking sea lieutenant assisted her to the deck. After the islander had been hoisted aboard in a chair, the rest of the party followed. While Block was describing their adventures to the lieutenant, Grace was politely conducted to the cabin. Here, she was gratified to find one of her own sex—the captain's niece, who was on her way to her home in New York, from a visit to cousins, daughters of the American Consul at Honolulu. The kind sympathy and frank but gentle manners of this young lady won the heart of our heroine at once. Before an hour had passed, each felt as though she had known the other for years.

CHAPTER IX.

" BLESS ME, I THOUGHT HE WAS A SAVAGE ! "

AFTER Block had concluded his story, quarters were selected for him in the steerage with the midshipmen, while his men were sent forward to mingle with the fore-mast hands. The islander had been carried to the cock-pit, and a surgeon was now dressing his wound.

Meanwhile, all sail having been crowded, the ship was howling along at the rate of nine knots in chase of the schooner. The character of this vessel was known to the captain of the pursuing craft almost at the moment when he first sighted her. From the skipper of a merchantman which arrived in the port of Honolulu previous to the departure of the sloop-of-war, he had obtained a good description of the pirate, by which his informant's vessel had been chased during its passage.

"Dear me!" cried the professor of languages, as he peered over the tall bulwarks at the fugitive craft, "I think we are gaining on her, and—"

He was interrupted by the thundering report of one of the ship's long "eighteen's," and the next moment he saw the schooner's mainmast go by the board.

"A good shot," remarked the captain, as he sprung upon a carronade slide and levelled his night-glass at the dismasted vessel, "that'll bring her to if her commander has common sense."

"Ay, ay, sir," responded the first lieutenant, "he can't hope to escape us after that. He is luffing up now, I think."

"You are right. But while some of his crew are clearing away the wreck, the rest are lowering the two boats. I don't understand that."

"It certainly looks queer, and if I'm not mistaken, he's bracing round his foreyards."

"Ay, ay, here the rascal comes, making straight for us, as if he were going to run into us!"

"He'll get the worst of the bargain, if he tries that foolish trick," exclaimed the lieutenant. "But look, sir, are not his men climbing over the bulwarks? I think I can see them."

"So they are. The rascals think to escape us by taking to their boats. Luff a little, quartermaster!"

"Luff it is, sir!"

"That will do—steady!"

"Steady she goes, sir!"

Scarcely had the deep-toned response died away, when a dense volume of smoke was seen to roll upward from one of the schooner's hatches, completely screening the boats from the watchful gaze of the ship's crew.

The pirates had set fire to their craft, not only to prevent its falling into the hands of their pursuers, but also to facilitate their escape; for, in order to keep clear of the burning vessel, the captain of the sloop-of-war would be obliged to keep off a point, thus affording his enemies a chance to get some distance to windward.

"That's a cunning trick," said the lieutenant, "and I'm afraid it'll prevent our capturing the rascals."

"I hardly think so," answered the captain, "we'll be after them on a taut bowline, as soon as we get astern of the schooner."

The lieutenant pointed out heavy masses of clouds which were drifting slowly towards the moon.

"It will soon be too dark to see the boats," said he.

"Ay, ay," the captain answered, impatiently, "I'm afraid you are right. Do you see them now?"

"I do. I can just make them out, far to windward of the burning craft."

This vessel was now about a quarter of a mile distant off the lee quarter. The flames had burst through her decks, and were shooting upward in long spiral columns, winding their fiery coils about her solitary mast and her fore-shrouds. Spreading rapidly, they soon covered every part of the doomed vessel, so that she looked like a floating pyramid of fire. The red glare of the conflagration, quivering upon the sky, and far along the waves, formed a singular contrast to the soft and peaceful radiance of the moon. The fore-shrouds of the ship were alive with spectators, among whom the green glasses of

Professor Quill, shining in the reflected light of the burning vessel, were so conspicuous as to attract considerable attention.

"My eyes, Bill," remarked one of the men to a shipmate, "that 'ere's the oddest lookin' lubber I ever did see. I wonder where he hails from ?"

"Don't know," replied Bill, "but his chum told me that he has lots of l'arnin'—enough to sink a seventy-four."

"Ay, ay, now, blow me, but I thought so !" exclaimed the other, "them that wears goggles always has l'arnin'. I never knowed it to fail yet."

"Dear me !" ejaculated the professor, at this juncture, "what a beautiful pyrotechnical display. I must describe it in my journal."

Bill and his chum exchanged glances, and nodded.

"Did you hear that, Tom ?" whispered the former, "did you hear that ? There's l'arnin' for you—pyro-tacknuckle !"

"Ay, ay, he's got the dictionary at his fingers' ends—he has," answered Tom. "And it's as well, mate," he added, solemnly, "for sich chaps as us not to be a-trying to repeat them big words after him."

"Why not ? That's the way to require l'arnin' ourselves."

Tom put one of his fingers upon the tip of his nose, and eyed his chum mysteriously.

"There was once upon a time," he whispered, "that my ideas was similar to your'n ; but that time's passed and gone, and it happened this way : When I was a-cruising in the Bombay, Captain Jenks, d'ye see, we had a chap named Munk for a shipmate, that was famous for his l'arnin', and another chap named Tom Tackle that

was'nt; a chap he was whose ignoramus was perfectly
wonderful. Being quite anxious-like, hows'ever, to require
l'arnin', he used to get Munk to speak long words for
him, and he'd speak 'em after him. Well, mate, one
day Munk gets off a mighty long word—a word as was
most astonishin', and would have made your hair stand
on end to hear. Open goes Tackle's mouth to repeat it
after him; but, my eyes! it was too much for him. He
sprung his jaw in trying so that he couldn't close his
mouth again, and his mouth has kept open ever since, a
living monument of the ambition of them that would
know more than their shipmates."

Before Tom could reply, a loud crash was heard, followed by a burst of admiration from Quill. The schooner's
foremast had fallen into the sea, and a shower of sparks
was now whirling upward from the roaring, crackling
waves of flame.

"Beautiful! beautiful!" cried the professor; "but it
will soon be over!"

"Ay, ay," exclaimed Block, "who had quitted the
steerage and mounted the fore shrouds, to obtain a good
view of the blazing craft. It will soon be over with the
schooner. The fire is involuntarily devouring every timber of the little vessel. Her dissolution is ineffable!"

"I tell you what it is, Bill," whispered Tom, "here's
some more l'arnin'."

"Why, yes," returned his chum. "Blow my eyes if I
don't think we've got into good company, and—"

He was interrupted by the order to "tack ship," and,
together with his shipmates, he quitted the shrouds and
sprung to the braces. The yards were soon hauled round,
and heading upon a course which would carry her astern
of the schooner, and in the track of the boats she rushed

through the water at the rate of eight knots. The crew then continued to watch the receding flames, until, having devoured nearly every plank and timber of the doomed craft, they went out among the waves of the sea.

"Ay, ay," muttered Block, "that's the last of her, and it's by no means inconsolable to see an institution of her character demoralised in this manner. Let all sinners take warnin' from the present statement of affairs, that they don't involve their heads in criminality."

"You are something of a philosopher, I perceive," observed a little midshipman at his elbow.

"Not exactly, my lad—not exactly. You've committed a sort of 'new-for-wrong' there, nat'ral to youngsters of your age. Though I may say, without comprehension, that I'm not wholly devoid of the 'promising spark,' yet I'm not much of a philosopher, except where women's consarned. The dictionary, hows'ever, is my principal 'forty.'"

The midshipman grinned.

"Perhaps you are enough of a philosopher," said he, "to tell me whether or not we'll succeed in capturing the boats to-night."

"Phrenologically considered," answered Block, striking an attitude, "I don't think we will. It's now as dark as pitch, and I think we're going to have a heavy gale. It's my opinion that the boats will get swamped."

Even as he spoke, the whistling of the blast was heard among the shrouds, and the ship suddenly keeled over to larboard. The pipe to furl sails was given, and was soon followed by the order to strike to'gallant yards and masts. The men flew to their stations with the activity of squirrels, and, in a short time, the vessel was ready to meet the full fury of the storm. Howling, roaring, and shrieking, it came at last, driving her through the water with terrific velocity, and whirling clouds of spray over her bulwarks. Her timbers groaned like human beings in mortal agony, her three masts swaying to and fro, creaked forth their complaints to the blast, while the seas, rising higher and higher every moment, came crashing and roaring over her weather-rail.

The gale continued to rage with great violence until daylight, when, the wind hauling round to the north'ard, it abated sufficiently to enable the ship to carry whole topsails. Midshipmen were then sent aloft with glasses, to look for the boats ; but after scrutinizing the sea in all directions, they reported nothing in sight.

"Ay, ay, the boats have been swamped beyond a doubt," said the captain, addressing his first lieutenant ; "they couldn't have lived in sucn a sea as that of last night. We may as well put the ship upon her course."

This was done, and, as the gale continued to abate, the vessel was soon bowling along under additional sail.

Before noon the wind had subsided to a moderate breeze, and the clouds having broken, the rays of the sun glittered brightly upon the crests of the heaving waves.

Then the two girls, Louisa and Grace, came on deck, and, taking a position near the weather quarter-rail, chatted pleasantly while watching the sea-birds skim over the tops and along the ridges of the rolling billows.

While thus occupied, they heard a step behind them, and turning, beheld the old surgeon, who had been to the cockpit, and was now proceeding toward the cabin. He politely lifted his cap and was passing on, when Grace ventured to inquire as to the condition of the invalid.

"He is getting on very well," replied the surgeon, "and I have no doubt that he will recover."

" Does he suffer much pain ? "

" Not a great deal."

" Is he able to speak ? "

" Oh, yes. I may add that I never before heard an islander speak so well. He inquired about you, and upon my informing him that you were safe and in good health, he seemed much pleased, and said that he would like to see you."

" And surely ! " cried Grace, impulsively, " he should not be denied this poor gratification."

A smile flitted for an instant across the face of the surgeon.

" It can do no harm," he said, after a moment's reflection, " so we will go to him at once."

" And I will go with you," said Louisa, " I feel much sympathy for the poor native."

To this he could make no objection, and so both girls were conducted to the cockpit.

Upon their entrance, the sufferer, who was lying in a rude bunk, turned his face toward them, when Grace uttered an exclamation of astonishment, for she recognized the well-known features of Guy Loring.

" Why ! How is this ? " murmured Louisa, in a low voice, " I thought he was a savage."

" And so he was, until this morning," replied the surgeon, smiling, and speaking in the same low tone, " when he called for soap and water, and, by washing the stains from his face, he transformed himself into a white man ; after which he informed me that his name was Guy Loring, and that he had been second mate of the Rainbow."

Louisa cast a shy glance at Grace from the corners of her eyes. The fair orphan had advanced to the side of the

wounded man, and, unknown to herself, there was a world
of pity and tenderness in her soft eyes as she looked down
upon his face.

"I never thought we should see you again," she faltered, "and, even now, I can hardly persuade myself
that I am not dreaming."

"And the surgeon did not deceive me. You are safe
—safe and well!" murmured Loring, his eyes shining
with pleasure.

"Yes, thanks to your brave exertions," she replied.
"You have acted nobly, and God will reward you. I owe
you a debt of gratitude which—"

"You owe me nothing," he interrupted, and the wistful
light now burning in his dark eyes covered her cheeks
with blushes. "You owe me nothing. Your safety is
my reward for what little I have done for you. Had you
been killed or injured, I could never have known a
moment's peace in this world. And now," he added,
changing the subject, "I owe you an explanation—"

"Not now—not now!" she cried; "wait until you are
stronger."

"Oh! no," he replied, "it does not hurt me to talk. My
story may be told in a few words."

Then, pausing a moment, as if to collect his thoughts,
he began the recital of his adventures since he parted from
his friends in the cutter. It shall be our task to take up
the thread of his narrative at the point where we left off
in a preceding chapter.

"My slumber," said he, "upon the mats in the chief-
tain's hut must have been very deep; for, when I awoke,
I discovered that my hands and feet were tied with ropes,
and that I was deprived of my clothing, for which was
substituted a piece of cloth fastened around my waist.

There was a smarting sensation about my cheeks and forehead, for which I could not account, until the same old woman of whom I have already spoken came to my side with a piece of looking-glass, and, stooping, held it before my eyes. To my astonishment, I perceived that my face was painted or rather stained in a hideous manner, being covered with circles, dots, squares, and crosses of blue and yellow. The old woman seemed to enjoy my consternation. She chuckled, grinned, and glared at me exultingly, pointing to my reflection in the glass, and screeching forth the word 'Loko,' several times, which I suppose was the new name by which I had been 'christened.' I was puzzled to account for the reason of my having been disfigured in the way I have mentioned, until I suddenly remembered that the Interpreter had informed me that it was the chief's intention to keep me for one of his warriors, and to prevent my being carried off by any of the white men who might visit the island. I raised myself upon my elbow and looked round for Mono, but he had gone. The hag and I were now the only persons in the hut. I glanced at the ropes around my wrists, and, by the manner in which they were tied, I felt sure that I could work my hands clear of them in the course of a few hours.

"And what then? The chances were ten to one that I would be recaptured if I attempted to escape, for the sound of voices without proclaimed that there were natives in the vicinity of the hut. Happening to glance toward the entrance, however, which commanded a view of the sea, I saw far away to the eastward, distinctly visible in the red light of the setting sun, a small speck, which I knew was a sail. This was encouraging, and the old woman, having now seated herself in her corner, I turned myself upon my side, and cautiously set about the task of freeing my hands. As I had supposed would be the case, I was several hours in accomplishing my purpose. Though the moon had, by this time, risen, yet the interior of the hut was quite dark, so that I was now able to free my ankles without being detected by my solitary guard. She had lighted her pipe, and a small stream of light enabled me to see her head, which was bowed upon her breast while she smoked. I sprung up, rushed past her, and ran toward the beach, where I hoped to fine a canoe; but I had not proceeded far, when I heard the cries of the old woman, followed by the yells of her savage brethren, who were now in pursuit of me.

" Having had the start, however, I gained the top of a bank which overlooked the beach while they were yet some distance behind. At the foot of the bank, to my unbounded astonishment, I beheld a female figure, and, the face being turned toward me, I recognized your features. You uttered a cry of terror—naturally supposing me to be a savage—and swooned. I picked you up, put you in a canoe, lying near the beach, and, springing in myself, paddled off toward the sail of which I have spoken. But being overtaken, notwithstanding my exertions, by the schooner—"

" That will do," Grace gently interrupted: " I know the rest."

He smiled, looked at her earnestly for a moment, and then closed his eyes in slumber.

" That's as it should be," whispered the surgeon. " I gave him an opiate when I visited him before."

" You are sure he will recover?"

" Oh! yes. He will be as well as he ever was in a few months."

As they emerged from the cockpit they encountered Block.

" Good morning, Miss Greenville," said he, " I am sincerely indisposed to meet with you. You will be disinterested to hear that we've just passed a capsized boat, which, it is my opinion, was one of them in which the pirates tried to escape from us, and the other one has probably suffered the same fatality."

" And I have news for you," said Grace, " which will doubtless please you very much. Your shipmate— Loring—is living. He and the savage in the cockpit are one and the same person."

" Why,—why—blow it !—excuse me—oh ! my eyes! no—you must be mistaken ; there must be some ' new-for-wrong ' about that !"

—" I have just left him asleep, below," answered Grace. " You will see him on deck before many weeks have passed."

In a few words she related the young man's adventures, to which Block listened with profound attention. When she had concluded, he drew a long breath, and struck the palm of his right hand with his clenched fist.

" It's parfectly wonderful !" he exclaimed. " I must pay him an invitation at once !"

" Some other time," said the good-natured surgeon ; " he is asleep now, and must not be disturbed."

The mate performed an awkward bow.

" Sartainly not ! The ' polytechnical ' usages of society must not be infringed into. I wish you a good-day while, I go and splice hands with my crew—that is the remains of 'em—over the good news."

So saying, he whirled round and made his way forward, in his haste nearly stumbling over the professor, who was seated upon a gun, very complacently sunning his green spectacles.

"Why, bless me!" he exclaimed, after Block had communicated his good news, "this is really quite astonishing and romantic. It must be put down in my journal at once!"

"I hope," said the mate, as the professor's pencil glided rapidly over the pages of the journal, pulled from beneath his jacket, "I hope you are in the habit of attenuating your phrases, so as not to make 'em too long."

The spectacles rattled: their owner began to sneeze violently, and, losing all patience, Block hurried off to seek the rest of his crew. He was not long in finding them, and great was their joy when the mate unfolded to them his budget of good news; for Loring had always been a favourite with his men.

CHAPTER X.

AS MIGHT BE EXPECTED.

THANKS to a good constitution, the second mate, in the course of a few weeks, was able to leave his bunk and make his way to the deck without assistance. The pure sea breeze aided him in recovering, and, ere long, the glow of health began to appear upon his brown cheek, while his eye grew brighter and his step more firm. Nevertheless, it was doubtful if he felt as happy now as he did while lying helpless in his berth, listening to the gentle voice of Grace Greenville, and basking, as it were, in the light of her soft brown eyes. With her friend Louisa, she had visited him many times, unconsciously winding about his heart a web of silvery network, from which it was destined never to escape. But now—now that he was strong enough to leave his couch and seek her, her manner toward him was singularly changed. She seemed rather to avoid him than otherwise, and whenever, as seldom happened, he did contrive to gain her ear, she was so shy and reserved, her responses were so few, and, as he chose to imagine, so cold, that he felt his heart sink within him. Unaccustomed to the gentler sex, he at length came to the conclusion that this reserve on her part proceeded from positive dislike of his society.

" Ay, ay, that's it," he muttered, to himself, one morning, as he stood in the lee gangway, with his eyes turned gloomily toward the quarter-deck from which she had just disappeared; " her sympathy for me during my illness was nothing more than what her kind little heart would have felt for any other sufferer. And now that I am well, she evidently wishes to have me understand that such was the case, and to discourage the hopes that I had formed. And what else should I expect? A rude, weather-beaten fellow like me, who has been tossed about by the sea ever since his boyhood! It would be unnatural that a gentle being like her should take any interest in a character of my stamp, and I have been very foolish building air-castles below there in my bunk. But I'll give 'em all up now—ay, ay. I'll give 'em all up, and may God bless the dear girl, and give her somebody more worthy of her than I am !"

" Disapp'inted affliction !" cried a voice behind him, " disapp'inted affliction, and nothing else !"

Loring turned to confront Block.

" I've overheard you, my lad," said that worthy, in a solemn voice; " every word; and allow me to inform you that you've been committing a great ' new-for-wrong' in not making me your confidential from the first ! "

"And why should I—"

"Why should you?" interrupted the mate; "why should you? This from my mate, whose obtuseness of intelligence I had 'flatuated' myself was nearly equal to my own! Why, my lad! you know what a parfect chronological I am about women don't ye? How I can divine 'em, and exterminate their smallest thoughts in the tyin' of a square knot, and how parfectly they are my 'forty,' to say nothing of the dictionary;—you know all this, don't ye?"

"I will not deny that I have heard Capstan say that you were a man of superior wisdom," Loring replied.

"Ay, ay," said Block, "Capstan depreciated my qualities through a sort of instinct nat'ral to men of his class. And now that he has imperceptibly vanished from this world of inquisitive criminality, it is my duty to instruct them that remains in something beside the hauling of a rope or the sarving of a shroud."

"Thank you," answered the second mate; "I am always glad to be instructed."

"Well, then, lad, as already through your discretion I have obtained a supreme glimpse into the symptoms of the mushroomery's daughter, allow me to state the fact that them women that seems cold is sometimes warm at heart, and them that seems warm is sometimes '*vicious varses.*'"

Loring's countenance brightened; observing which, the first mate placed one of his great horny fingers upon the side of his club nose and groaned:—

"Don't look that way, lad! don't look that way," he cried, "for it goes ag'in my grain to intersperse false hopes in the hearts of them that's smitten. I didn't mean, by what I said, to exhilarate in your mind the idea that the girl is favourable. No, not by any means. Women is hard to divine, and Miss Grace isn't an 'acceptation.' I have often watched her while you was exarting your conversational liabilities with her, and I must acknowledge that there wasn't nothing about her ways to warrant the presumption of love. I may add, that it is my candid superstition her afflictions is preoccupied with the second officer of this craft, with which I have seen her talking more than once, and—ay, there they are now!" he suddenly interrupted.

Loring turned to witness a spectacle that sent a sharp pang to his heart. Near the weather-rail stood Grace, conversing with the second lieutenant, a tall, handsome, man, whose fine figure was set off to advantage by his neat uniform. The young girl seemed—at least, so thought Loring—much pleased with her stately companion. A continual smile played about her lips, and once she even broke forth into a silvery peal of laughter at some witty remark on his part. Suddenly, however, she glanced toward the spot occupied by Loring. She coloured deeply; the smile faded from her lips; she became quite grave, and all the efforts of her companion to amuse her seemed now of no avail.

"She is angry because she saw me watching them," thought Loring, and turning sadly away, he walked off to another part of the ship.

"Ay, ay," muttered Block, looking after him, "it's a clean case of disapp'inted affliction—a decided 'new-for wrong,' and it'll be more 'disapp'intedest' yet before it's all over. Poor lad—poor lad! I never saw his equal in handling a marlingspike and splicing a brace; yet them qualities are too modest to perspire to the hand of that lass. It's a pity they ever met!"

At that moment, a shrill warning cry came down from aloft, penetrating every corner of the ship.

"Look out there, below—on deck—look out!" and glancing upward, the quick eye of the mate at once detected the cause of the alarm.

A new studding-sail-boom, which was being hoisted to the maintopsail yard, was fast working clear of the rope to which it was attached; so that there was every probability of its falling to the deck before any measures could be taken to prevent the accident.

Startled by the warning shriek that pierced her brain like a knife, and imagining that some great catastrophe was about to happen, such as the falling of the masts, or perhaps even the foundering of the ship, Grace Greenville sprang from the quarter-deck, and fled instinctively to the side of Guy for protection. At the same instant, down came the boom, crashing to the deck, one end of it striking the main fife-rail, and breaking a couple of belaying-pins.

The second mate then conducted the trembling girl back to the quarter-deck, which was now deserted by the ship's officers, who had gone to reprimand the sailor whose carelessness in hitching the rope was the cause of the accident.

"I am ashamed of myself," said Grace, "for being so easily frightened."

"It was perfectly natural that you were," replied Loring, "and I may add, that I feel proud and happy because you came to me for protection. It has inspired me with a hope that perhaps you do not dislike me as much as I had supposed."

She gave him a timid, reproachful glance.

"I was not aware," she said, in a low but earnest voice,

"that I ever gave you any reason to suppose that I dis-
liked you. Far from it, I esteem you very much."

"Bless you for the words!" cried Loring, impulsively,
lifting her hand to his lips, "for they have made me a
happy man. Ay, ay," he added, gazing tenderly upon her
partially averted face, "a happy man, for, though I am
a rude sailor, I have dared to love you. You are dearer,
far dearer, than all the world to me, and I frankly ask
you—feeling at the same time that I am not worthy of
such an angel—whether, after what I have said, you will
allow me to come and see you after we arrive at New
York?"

She did not speak, but her hand dropped as lightly as
a snow-flake into his; a tender glance beamed upon him
from her soft brown eyes, and the next moment she had
disappeared through the companionway.

A few months later, on a clear sunny morning, the
sloop-of-war came to an anchor off the Battery, and
before noon Grace was in the arms of her aunt, who
occupied a neat cottage in the upper part of the city.
The second mate called there on the next day, and was
cordially welcomed by the old lady, to whom, while
relating her perils, the niece had not failed to praise the
conduct of her noble lover.

About six weeks after, while seated in a saloon poring
over the columns of a daily paper, Block was astonished
to find in the marriage list the names of Grace Greenville
and Guy Loring.

"Why! this is perfectly wonderful!" he exclaimed,
springing to his feet, "to read of them two being spliced!
Ay, ay, and for once in my life, I've committed a 'new-
for-wrong' in the divining of a woman. I have been

deceived in thinking that she was afflicted with that second lieutenant of the sloop-of-war!"

Subsequently, the marriage notice was also seen by the professor of languages, who now occupied an apartment in the St. Nicholas Hotel.

"Why, dear me!" he exclaimed, carefully adjusting the green spectacles to make sure that his eyes did not deceive him, "this will really make quite an item for my journal! I must finish it, and look up a publisher as soon as possible!"

Alas! it never was finished! The professor was so particular about his language, that he kept revising and improving the journal for ten years, at the end of which time he died—long before he had brought the work to the coveted state of perfection!

A few days after his burial, a little girl of eight years, came to plant flowers over his grave. She was a very pretty, interesting child, with bright golden hair hanging in curls about her face and neck, and with large soft brown eyes. Now and then, while occupied with her simple task, she would pause to listen to the song of a bird, which, from its position upon the bough of a willow-tree, near the tombstone, seemed to watch her with much attention.

"Who knows," she muttered to herself, after she had looked at it several times, "who knows but that's Uncle Quill, come to see what I'm about. Mamma says that when people die they go to the spirit land; but I shouldn't wonder if God let's 'em come back to the earth sometimes in different shapes than when they went away. Uncle Quill wore green spectacles when he went away, but of course he couldn't wear 'em if he's a bird. If this is he, he'll be very glad to see me planting these flowers over his grave. I can't help thinking it is he, for it keeps saying, " Dear me ! dear me !" and Uncle Quill was always saying that ! I—"

Hearing footsteps approaching, she paused abruptly, and rose to her feet. A rough-looking sailor, wearing a canvas jacket, a huge glazed sou'wester, and a pair of duck pants, emerged from behind a clump of shrubbery, and moved toward her. Frightened by his weather-beaten face, which was disfigured by a nose of enormous proportions, she turned to run, but was checked by his voice.

" Avast there, little gal !" he exclaimed, " it's a decided ' new-for-wrong '— your running away from me. I wouldn't hurt ye for the world. You are one of the most inimical little fairies I ever saw, and your sex is my ' forty,' and has been ever since I buried my three wives ! I've been a watching ye for some time, from behind yonder bit of shrubbery, and there's a familiar item in your looks that has excited my disinterestedness in a manner which I may say is highly ingenious."

He was now in front of her, and, stooping, he clasped her hand in his great horny palm. She trembled, and glanced timidly up into his face.

" I've seen ye before," he continued ; " to speak more chronologically, I've seen somebody that bore a striking resemblance to your pretty figure-head ! It was years ago, aboard a merchantman of which I was mate. The one I have realization to was a young gal—one of the loveliest, and at the same time one of the most unper-spicuous of her sex. She was the only one of her sex who ever ruffled my penetration. She deceived me mightily, she did, with regard to her afflictions, which I thought was concentrated in the lieutenant of a sloop-of-

war, when in reality they was emerged in my second mate,
Guy Loring."

"Why, that's papa's name !" cried the little girl, clapping her hands, and laughing delightedly.   "I have
heard papa speak of a Mr. Block, and—"

"Which means me !" interrupted the mate, slapping
the tombstone with his disengaged palm.   "Ay ay, and
this is a happy meeting : it's what I call sarcumstantial
evidence.   I've been a hunting up your father and mother
for the last three days ; having come home from a long
v'yage a week ago ! And—why shiver me little gal ! what
does this mean " he suddenly added, as his glance suddenly
fell upon the inscription on the tombstone, " here's the
name of one of my crew of the old Rainbow !   It isn't
possible though, that—"

" Uncle Quill was buried here !" interrupted the little
girl ; " he was a real nice man, and used to come to see
us very often.   I liked him very much, and so did brother
Robert, and Tommy, and Harry, and—"

" Avast ! avast there, little gal ! You don't mean to
say that so many little jolly-boats has sprung up already
around your father and mother !   You don't mean to say
that there are more than three of ye ?"

" There are five," answered the child, " counting the
baby."

Block placed a finger upon the end of his nose, and gave
vent to a shrill, prolonged whistle, which so startled his
little companion, that she made a movement as if she
would run away.

" Hold on fairy !" he exclaimed, " don't be frightened.
You took away my breath, that was all, seeing as the
three Mrs. Blocks altogether wasn't half as lucky as them
that's your parents.   Ay, ay," he continued, as he again

looked at the tombstone, "that was the name of one of my crew, but if it's your uncle, I—"

"Oh, no !" interrupted the child, "he wasn't our real uncle. We haven't any real uncle, but we called him so because we liked him so much, and because he wore green spectacles !"

"That was him ! that was the professor, sure enough !" cried Block, emphatically, "there's no mistake upon that p'int. And so he's dead—the professor is dead ! I always thought he'd die an 'arly death, as too much l'arnin' makes a man top-heavy !" saying which, the mate felt his own rough head, and moved it up and down in a reflective manner.

"Have you got the headache ?" the child anxiously inquired, looking up ; "I hope you haven't, Mr. Block, I hope—"

"Oh, no," interrupted the mate, "I was only a-thinkin' that, to use a clerical impression, I too might soon be a going, as the pile of eddicated dictionary tarms in my brain is so enormous that they can never evaporate ! But come," he added, rubbing his club nose energetically, as though he would thus dissipate his gloomy thoughts, "you must pilot me to your parents' house, little one, where I hope we'll have a pleasant time talking over our antiquated times !"

Accordingly the little girl led the way from the grave-yard, and along a narrow road bordered by oaks and button-wood trees of gigantic growth. The sun had nearly set, and the red light streaming through the branches and leaves fell softly upon the golden hair of the child, and seemed to encircle it with a halo of glory. She ran on ahead of her follower with the buoyant step of health, and soon arrived before the gate of a tasteful-looking building of cedar-wood, and half-buried in clambering vines and flowers.   Seated upon a balcony in front were Grace and her husband, the former looking lovelier even than she did ten years previously, and the latter also much improved.   Guy was reading a newspaper, and his handsome wife was playing with a chubby little infant upon her lap, while other children sported around her chair.

"Oh ma! oh, papa!" shouted Block's little pilot, running towards the piazza, here is Mr. Block come to see you.   The same Mr. Block that you've spoken about so much!"

With a bound, Guy sprang into the yard, and seizing the mate's hand with a true sailor grasp, shook it heartily, while he shouted a joyful welcome to his old messmate. Grace seemed equally glad to see him, and forgetting his dignity as a man of profound erudition, Block unconsciously danced a sort of hornpipe, as he fixed his admiring eyes upon the young matron.

"Ay, ay!" he exclaimed, roaring with delighted laughter.   "Ay, ay, here we three are again once more reunited as we was aboard the merchantman and sloop-of-war.   The ways of Providence is truly unscrupulous and divine.   Why, Miss Grace—or Mrs. Grace, as I should now say—you improve with age, like a bottle of wine, though you ain't so very old neither—not half as old as either of the Mrs. Blocks was when she died.   Long life to ye, say I, and long life to the little jolly-boats and all. Blow me, Loring, but this incongruous tempting display that I see around me—them little rosy children, and you and your wife, which I am now introducing upon—have somehow set my head in a whirl, and made me think of taking a fourth Mrs. Block!"

"I should advise you to do so by all means!" laughed Guy. "Your own experience must tell you that there is nothing like marriage to cure a man of his roving propensities!"

"Ay, ay, chum, you are right there! I need an ingenious companion to settle me down, and I shall sartainly take your advice."

The mate kept his word. After passing three pleasant days with Guy and his wife, he took his departure, and making his way to the town of Jamaica with all possible speed, proposed to a little widow who had once rejected him on account of his enormous nose, but who now, with the unaccountable capriciousness of her sex, accepted him without hesitation. She made him a good wife, and in due course of time presented him with a pair of little twin Blocks. The nose of each was clubbed like that of the father, and the latter was much pleased to trace other points of resemblance to himself in the faces of the two.

When they became old enough to read, their father purchased a huge English dictionary, and ordered them to study it until they had mastered all the long and high-sounding words it contained. Accordingly, the little Blocks applied themselves diligently to their task, and by the time they were ten years of age, their remarkable precocity was the talk of the whole neighbourhoood. Hopping like little toads around the chairs of elderly visitors, they would astonish the latter by uttering such words as "philosophical," "propugnation," "proselytism," "pyrotechnist," and—

"FINIS."

24 AU 66

LONDON: W. J. JOHNSON, PRINTER, 121, FLEET STREET.

ROUTLEDGE'S SHILLING NOVELS.

By J. FENIMORE COOPER.

In fcp. 8vo, fancy covers, 1s. each.

THE PILOT.
THE PIONEERS.
THE DEERSLAYER.
LIONEL LINCOLN.
THE BRAVO.
THE TWO ADMIRALS.
THE WATERWITCH.
WYANDOTTE.
MILES WALLINGFORD.
THE PRAIRIE.
THE HEATHCOTES.
PRECAUTION.
MARK'S REEF.
THE LAST OF THE MOHICANS.
THE SPY.
THE PATHFINDER.
THE RED ROVER.
THE HEIDENMAUER.
SATANSTOE.
AFLOAT AND ASHORE.
EVE EFFINGHAM.
THE HEADSMAN.
HOMEWARD BOUND.
THE SEA LIONS.
OAK OPENINGS.
NED MYERS.

GEORGE ROUTLEDGE & SONS, Broadway, Ludgate Hill.

ROUTLEDGE'S SHILLING NOVELS.

By G. P. R. JAMES.

In fcp. 8vo, fancy covers, 1s. each.

THE BRIGAND.
DARNLEY.
THE WOODMAN.
MORLEY ERNSTEIN.
THE GIPSY.
HENRY OF GUISE.
ATTILA.
ARABELLA STUART.
AGINCOURT.
RUSSELL; OR, THE RYE HOUSE PLOT.
THE KING'S HIGHWAY.
THE CASTLE OF EHREN-STEIN.
THE STEPMOTHER.
FOREST DAYS; OR, ROBIN HOOD.
THE HUGUENOT.
THE MAN AT ARMS,
A WHIM AND ITS CONSE-QUENCES.
HENRY MASTERTON.
THE CONVICT.
MARY OF BURGUNDY.
MARGARET GRAHAM.
GOWRIE; OR, THE KING'S PLOT.

DELAWARE.
DARK SCENES OF HIS-TORY.
THE ROBBER.
ONE IN A THOUSAND.
THE SMUGGLER.
RICHELIEU.
DE LORME.
ARRAH NEIL.
BEAUCHAMP.
CASTELNEAU.
THE FALSE HEIR.
THF FORGERY.
THE GENTLEMAN OF THE OLD SCHOOL.
HEIDELBERG.
THE JACQUERIE.
MY AUNT PONTYPOOL
ROSE D'ALBRET.
SIR THEODORE BROUGH-TON.
CHARLES TYRRELL.
JOHN MARSTON HALL.
PHILIP AUGUSTUS.
THE BLACK EAGLE.
LEONORA D'ORCO.
THE OLD DOMINION.

GEORGE ROUTLEDGE & SONS, Broadway, Ludgate Hill.

ROUTLEDGE'S SHILLING NOVELS.

By W. HARRISON AINSWORTH.

WINDSOR CASTLE.

THE MISER'S DAUGHTER.

THE TOWER OF LONDON.

CRICHTON.

JAMES THE SECOND.

OLD ST. PAUL'S.

THE FLITCH OF BACON.

GUY FAWKES.

THE LANCASHIRE WITCHES.

MERVYN CLITHEROE.

OVINGDEAN GRANGE.

ROOKWOOD.

ST. JAMES'S; OR, THE COURT OF QUEEN ANNE.

THE SPENDTHRIT.

THE STAR CHAMBER.

AURIOL.

JACK SHEPPARD.

GEORGE ROUTLEDGE & SONS, Broadway, Ludgate Hill.

ROUTLEDGE'S SHILLING NOVELS.

By CAPTAIN MARRYAT.

In fscp. 8vo, fancy covers, 1s. each.

PETER SIMPLE.

JACOB FAITHFUL.

NEWTON FORSTER.

THE PACHA OF MANY TALES.

PERCIVAL KEENE.

JAPHET IN SEARCH OF A FATHER.

FRANK MILDMAY.

MR. MIDSHIPMAN EASY.

THE POACHER.

VALERIE.

THE KING'S OWN.

RATTLIN THE REEFER.

THE PHANTOM SHIP.

THE DOG FIEND.

MISCELLANEOUS.

1s. each.

NOTHING BUT MONEY. By T. S. ARTHUR.

THE FAMILY FEUD. By THOMAS COOPER.

ADELAIDE LINDSAY. By the Author of "EMILIA WYNDHAM."

THE LITTLE WIFE. By Mrs. GREY.

RITA: An AUTOBIOGRAPHY.

LILLY DAWSON. By Mrs. CROWE.

THE HENPECKED HUSBAND. By LADY SCOTT.

WHOM TO MARRY. By MAYHEW.

TOUGH YARNS. By the "OLD SAILOR."

GEORGE ROUTLEDGE & SONS, Broadway, Ludgate Hill.

JAMES GRANT'S NOVELS.

THE ROMANCE OF WAR; or, The Highlanders in Spain.

THE AIDE-DE-CAMP.

THE SCOTTISH CAVALIER.

BOTHWELL.

JANE SETON; or, The Queen's Advocate.

PHILIP ROLLO.

LEGENDS OF THE BLACK WATCH.

MARY OF LORRAINE.

OLIVER ELLIS; or, The Fusiliers.

LUCY ARDEN; or, Hollywood Hall.

FRANK HILTON; or, The Queen's Own.

THE YELLOW FRIGATE.

HARRY OGILVIE; or, The Black Dragoons.

ARTHUR BLANE.

LAURA EVERINGHAM; or, The Highlanders of Glenora.

THE CAPTAIN OF THE GUARD.

LETTY HYDE'S LOVERS.

CAVALIERS OF FORTUNE.

SECOND TO NONE.

THE CONSTABLE OF FRANCE.

The above in Cloth Gilt, 2s. 6d. each.

GEORGE ROUTLEDGE & SONS, Broadway, Ludgate Hill.

BULWER LYTTON'S WORKS.

CHEAP EDITION, in fscp. 8vo, Boards,

Price 2s. each.

A STRANGE STORY.
WHAT WILL HE DO WITH IT? Vol. 1.
WHAT WILL HE DO WITH IT? Vol. II.
PELHAM.
PAUL CLIFFORD.
EUGENE ARAM.
THE LAST DAYS OF POMPEII.
THE LAST OF THE BARONS.
RIENZI.
ERNEST MALTRAVERS.
ALICE.
NIGHT AND MORNING.
THE DISOWNED.
DEVEREUX.
THE CAXTONS.
MY NOVEL. Vol. I.
MY NOVEL. Vol. II.
LUCRETIA.
HAROLD.

Price 1s. 6d. each.

GODOLPHIN. | ZANONI.

Price 1s. each.

THE PILGRIMS OF THE RHINE.
LEILA; OR, THE SIEGE OF GRANADA.

GEORGE ROUTLEDGE & SONS, Broadway, Ludgate Hill.

www.ingramcontent.com/pod-product-compliance
Lightning Source LLC
LaVergne TN
LVHW061218060426
835508LV00014B/1349